Fingerpicking
Techniques
for Guitar

Fingerpicking
Techniques *for* Guitar

PHIL CAPONE

APPLE

A QUARTO BOOK
FINGERPICKING TECHNIQUES
FOR GUITAR

First published in 2010 by
Apple Press
7 Greenland Street
London NW1 0ND
www.apple-press.com

QUAR. AFSB
ISBN: 978-1-84543-361-1

Conceived, designed and
produced by
Quarto Publishing plc
The Old Brewery
6 Blundell Street
London N7 9BH

Project Editor: Emma Poulter
Art Editor: Elizabeth Healey
Design Assistant: Saffron Stocker
Photographer: Martin Norris
Copy Editor: Sally MacEachern
Proofreader: Claire Waite Brown
Indexer: Dorothy Frame
Art Director: Caroline Guest
Creative Director: Moira Clinch
Publisher: Paul Carslake

CD envelope by Modern Age
Repro House Ltd, Hong Kong
Printed by Midas Printing
International Ltd, China

Contents

Introduction   6
About this book   8
The fingerboard   10
Notes for left-handed players   12

Chapter 1: The Lessons   14
Lesson 1: Reading the dots   16
Lesson 2: How to hold your guitar   18
Lesson 3: Tune up   20
Lesson 4: The right-hand position   22
Lesson 5: The left-hand position   24
Lesson 6: Playing bass notes   26
Lesson 7: Adding melody notes   30
Lesson 8: Open chord shapes   34
Lesson 9: Three easy pieces   38
Lesson 10: Syncopated patterns   44
Lesson 11: Moveable chord shapes   50
Lesson 12: Transposing patterns   54
Lesson 13: Semiquaver patterns   60
Lesson 14: Barre chord patterns   66
Lesson 15: Roots and fifths   72
Lesson 16: Country workout   78
Lesson 17: Alternating thumb bass   88
Lesson 18: Homesick Blues   94
Lesson 19: Harmonizing major melodies   102
Lesson 20: Morning Has Broken   108

Lesson 21: Harmonizing minor melodies   116
Lesson 22: Scarborough Fair   126
Lesson 23: Playing riffs   134
Lesson 24: The Gallows Pole   140
Lesson 25: Major sevenths and exotic
            dominant chords   148
Lesson 26: Latin American rhythms   152
Lesson 27: Latin workout   158
Lesson 28: Playing tenths   168
Lesson 29: Walking basslines   176

Chapter 2: Picking Pattern Directory   **182**

Chapter 3: Capo Keys   **230**
First fret keys   232
Second fret keys   234
Third fret keys   236
Fourth fret keys   238
Fifth fret keys   240
Sixth fret keys   242
Seventh fret keys   244
Eighth fret keys   246
Ninth fret keys   248

Glossary   250
Index   253
Credits   256

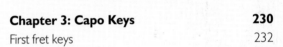

Introduction

Fingerpicking is not the easiest of guitar techniques to master, but ultimately it's much more rewarding than, say, just strumming out a few chords. Some might say that fingerpicking is beyond the scope of a regular "teach yourself" manual and demands a personal tutor; but this is no regular "teach yourself" manual. Each lesson is clearly presented and explained using text, photographs and easy-to-follow notation (both conventional and TAB). An accompanying CD lets you hear exactly how each piece should sound. In short, if you want to learn how to fingerpick, this book will show you how – and at your own pace. It will also save you a small fortune in private tuition fees!

The 29 lessons take you from the basics (tuning, how to hold the guitar, hand positions, etc.) to exciting arrangements of traditional and original tunes. The refreshingly breezy style of the text makes each lesson a joy rather than a chore; no more boring monologue, just fun pieces to play! A selection of picking patterns that can be applied to a wide range of styles is included in the supplementary Picking Pattern Directory. Each pattern comes complete with a detailed description, performance notes, a suggested chord progression and an easy-to-read "finger and string sequence" pattern, unique to this book. Finally, the fingerpicker's favourite tool, the capo. An explanation of its merits is followed by a reference section that illustrates how to play in any key using just a handful of open chords and a capo. Once again, this is a useful and informative resource that you won't find in any other fingerpicking book.

And, maybe best of all, its handy compact form makes the book "guitar case friendly", so you can take it with you wherever you go. The spiral binding allows you to open it out flat, making it a pleasure to use – and guaranteed to make your practice sessions productive. So, grab your guitar and let's get started...

About this book

The ultimate companion for guitarists, this book assumes a basic level of proficiency, but caters for both the novice and experienced player, and is perfect for those wanting to build up their right-hand ability to play a range of musical styles.

The Lessons (pages 14–181)

This chapter is devoted to a series of lessons that will show you how to use fingerpicking techniques to unlock the secrets of some of the most iconic sounds in the guitar repertoire.

The lessons are taught through a series of exercises that are demonstrated on the accompanying audio CD. This makes it easy to understand what you can achieve and provides a goal for practice, since it illustrates how finished pieces should sound.

Each lesson's content is broken up with helpful "Top tips" that highlight important techniques or approaches and explain them.

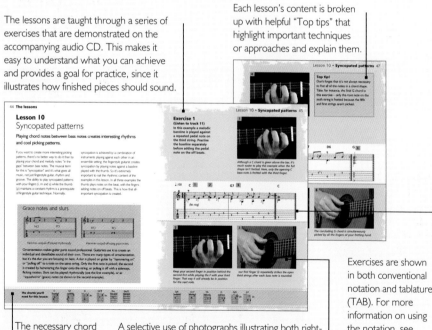

Exercises are shown in both conventional notation and tablature (TAB). For more information on using the notation, see Lesson 1: Reading the dots (pages 18–19).

The necessary chord shapes are called out diagrammatically at the beginning of each lesson.

A selective use of photographs illustrating both right-hand and left-hand techniques and fingering detail adds clarity where required. These photographs are numbered to the musical notation.

Picking Pattern Directory (pages 182–229)

Here you'll find a fantastic compilation of picking patterns that can be used to create instant accompaniments.

For the first half of the patterns, the chord shapes are shown photographically to help you on your way, and in a simplified, diagrammatic format thereafter.

A brief description of each pattern's merits, technical demands and suggested uses is given.

Each pattern is notated in three ways: with conventional notation, TAB and – unique to this book – an easy-to-read "finger and string sequence" diagram. Right-hand fingering is indicated using traditional Spanish abbreviations p, i, m, a (see page 23).

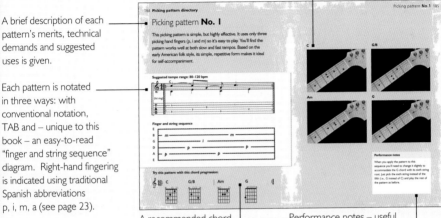

A recommended chord sequence to try the pattern with is provided.

Performance notes – useful tips and suggestions – are also provided to enable you to get the most out of these patterns.

Capo Keys (pages 230–249)

This invaluable resource helps you to find the best fretboard location for your chosen key using the capo and open chord shapes.

Capo key positions and the open chord regions are shown diagrammatically.

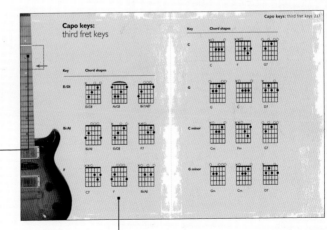

The keys available on any given fret are provided.

The fingerboard

Finding notes on the fingerboard isn't easy; even accomplished players can be sketchy on this knowledge if they've learnt primarily "by ear." This easy-to-use diagram will help you locate any note – and fast! Remember that after the twelfth fret the entire fingerboard repeats an octave higher (starting with the open string note name).

Fret 1
6 – F
5 – A♯/B♭
4 – D♯/E♭
3 – G♯/A♭
2 – C
1 – F

Fret 2
6 – F♯/G♭
5 – B
4 – E
3 – A
2 – C♯
1 – F♯/G♭

Fret 3
6 – G
5 – C
4 – F
3 – A♯/B♭
2 – D
1 – G

Fret 4
6 – G♯/A♭
5 – C♯/D♭
4 – F♯/G♭
3 – B
2 – D♯/E♭
1 – G♯/A♭

FINGERBOARD REPETITION
The twelfth fret is the same as the open strings – from then on the notes repeat. For example fret 13 is the same as fret 1.

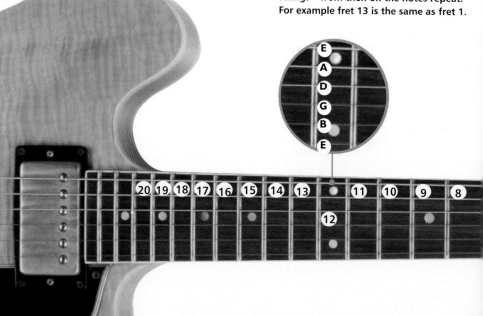

Fret 5
6 – A
5 – D
4 – G
3 – C
2 – E
1 – A

Fret 7
6 – B
5 – E
4 – A
3 – D
2 – F♯
1 – B

Fret 9
6 – C♯/D♭
5 – F♯/G♭
4 – B
3 – E
2 – G♯/A♭
1 – C♯/D♭

Fret 11
6 – D♯/E♭
5 – G♯/A♭
4 – C♯/D♭
3 – F♯/G♭
2 – A♯/B♭
1 – D♯/E♭

Fret 6
6 – A♯/B♭
5 – D♯/E♭
4 – G♯/A♭
3 – C♯/D♭
2 – F
1 – A♯/B♭

Fret 8
6 – C
5 – F
4 – A♯/B♭
3 – D♯/E♭
2 – G
1 – C

Fret 10
6 – D
5 – G
4 – C
3 – F
2 – A
1 – D

Fret 12
6 – E
5 – A
4 – D
3 – G
2 – B
1 – E

OPEN STRINGS AND BARRE CHORDS
When a string is included in a chord without being fretted it is called an "open string", indicated on the chord diagram by a "O". Strings not included at all are called out with an "X". Where two notes are joined by a bracket on the diagram, a barre chord should be played.

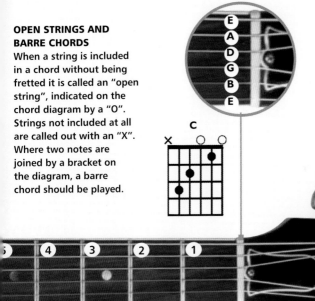

Notes for left-handed players

The aspiring left-handed guitarist has a dilemma to face: is it best to buy a left-handed instrument, or simply to play right-handed and enjoy the wider choice (and often lower prices) of instruments available to "righties"?

Left v right

On a conventional guitar, the fingerpicking hand is the right hand. This can prove problematic for left-handed players. Some "lefties" will simply opt to play a right-handed guitar. After all, there is no such thing as a left-handed piano. Try a few left-handed and right-handed guitars in a music store before you make your decision. Don't worry if you can't play anything; just sit down with the instrument and pick a couple of open strings. If a left-handed instrument feels more natural to hold, then go with your gut feeling. There are plenty of famous left-handed guitarists (Sir Paul McCartney for starters) so you won't be alone if you choose a left-handed model. These are available across all the major manufacturers' ranges.

Adapting a right-handed guitar

The alternative is to buy a right-handed guitar, flip it upside down, and re-string it, but this can cause intonation and tuning problems and you may find it awkward to play when sitting. Furthermore, the cutaway of an electric guitar will be on the wrong side of the neck, making access to high notes difficult. In the long run, it's less hassle to buy a left-handed guitar: all of the key components (the bridge, nut, body and neck) are reversed to ensure the instrument is comfortable to play and easy to tune. But there are no hard and fast rules. Some players learn to play a right-handed guitar turned upside down without re-stringing! With the high G string closest to you, everything is, in effect, back to front!

Paul McCartney would play both a genuine left-handed guitar or, as pictured, a right-handed instrument altered for left-handed playing.

Using this book

As far as reading music goes, the pitches on the stave or TAB don't relate to the guitar visually, so this should present no real problems. Scale and arpeggio diagrams are a little trickier since you will have to reverse the shape or pattern. Don't worry "lefties": this is not as complicated as it sounds and, with a little practice, you will soon be able to decipher these diagrams with no real difficulty.

THE LESSONS

This chapter consists of a series of exercises that will teach you all of the skills you'll need to become a proficient fingerstyle guitarist. The lessons are progressive and designed to build your technique gradually while you play. Don't be tempted to skip chapters; you'll achieve the best results by working through the lessons sequentially. Every single exercise and arrangement has been specifically designed to make the learning process an exciting and enjoyable one; you'll find no boring scales and arpeggios here!

To get the most out of this book, you should aim to review the previous lessons as often as you can, preferably at the start of every practice session. This will reinforce your knowledge and boost your confidence; you'll be wowing your friends with your newfound musical talents in no time!

Lesson 1
Reading the dots

Even if you can already read TAB, this introduction will help you get the most out of every lesson.

Every example in this book has been annotated using a combination of conventional notation (what musos call "the dots") and TAB (short for "tablature"). This is the standard that's used by most guitar publications today. You'll find this convention everywhere, from the songbooks of your favourite bands to the transcriptions in leading guitar magazines. Although it's

not necessary to be a fluent sight reader to get the most from this book, you'll find that conventional notation is extremely useful in two essential areas: for describing rhythmic content and for differentiating between melody notes and bass notes in fingerstyle arrangements (i.e., those notes you play with your fingers and those you play with your thumb – more on this later).

Example 1

The traditional five-line stave is not guitar specific; it's used for any instrument that reads from the treble clef. (Some instruments read from

different clefs that change the range of notes on the stave.) Each line and space has a corresponding letter name that represents a musical note.

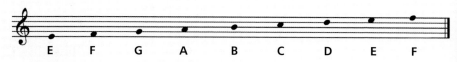

Example 2

In this example you can see how the six lines of the TAB stave represent the six strings of the guitar, starting with the lowest (E) at the bottom. To read

TAB all you have to do is convert the number on the line to a fret on the corresponding string – easy!

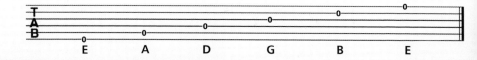

Example 3

A stave of conventional notation has been added above the TAB stave. You can see how easy it is to find the notes from example 1 when the conventional notation has a stave of TAB added below it.

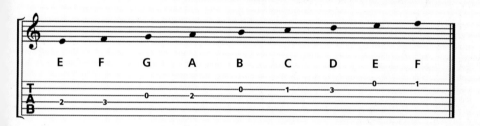

Example 4

Here you can see how the notes written in conventional notation describe duration (i.e. rhythm) as well as pitch. With a little practice you'll soon be able to identify rhythms on sight.

Example 5

For each of the notes in example 4 there's an equivalent rest. Don't forget it's not what you play, but what you leave out that counts!

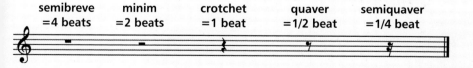

Lesson 2
How to hold your guitar

Time spent on achieving correct posture, whether you're sitting or standing, is time well spent.

Bad posture can cause muscular problems; it also makes practising a chore because you won't feel relaxed. It's really important to feel comfortable when you're practising; it should be an enjoyable experience where the music takes you to other places. Practising can be as deeply rewarding as meditation, but only if you're not suffering from aches and pains caused by bad posture. Most players practice while sitting down, simply because it's more comfortable over long periods of time. Some electric players like to use a strap, even when they're sitting down. This is because it raises the height of the instrument and helps spread the weight (solid-bodied electrics can be heavy). For acoustic players this is less likely to be an issue, but you may still want to try sitting with a strap just to experiment. If it feels good, do it!

Try to avoid hunching over the guitar, and keep your legs uncrossed. Place the guitar with the curved, indented underside of the body over your right thigh and the headstock pointing to the left.

When you are sitting correctly, the back of the guitar should be in contact with your stomach.

The guitar neck should be roughly parallel with the floor.

Top tip!

Take time to correct your posture and make sure you are comfortable with your guitar. An awkward playing position makes practising hard work, meaning you'll spend less time with your instrument.

Experiment with your strap and keep adjusting it until you're comfortable. There's no optimum position; this varies from player to player, but avoid wearing the guitar too low – it may look cool but it's really bad news for your fretting hand. Above, fingerpicking Joan Baez wears a strap tailored for comfort.

Lesson 3
Tune up

An out-of-tune guitar will make you sound bad, so it's well worth taking time out to learn how to tune efficiently.

Many guitarists think that tuning is a chore and should only be performed occasionally – wrong! Guitar strings are under a lot of stress, so even a top quality instrument won't stay in tune for long. Get into the habit of checking your tuning every time you pick up your guitar.

Tuning by ear

This method is called "relative tuning" since it only verifies that the guitar is in tune with itself (as opposed to concert pitch). Using the TAB below you can check each pair of strings, starting with the lowest. Each pair of notes produces the pitch indicated above the TAB, so play the strings simultaneously for best results. When the pitches are close you will hear a beating or pulsating effect caused by the slight difference in pitch. As the pitches get closer the beating slows; it disappears when the strings are in tune.

Using a tuner

An electronic tuner will keep your guitar in concert pitch. This is not only important when you play with other musicians; it also keeps the strings at their correct tension. If the strings are too tight or too loose your guitar's neck could be damaged. Electric guitars (or acoustic guitars fitted with a pick-up) can be plugged directly into a tuner. Most tuners also have a built-in microphone for tuning acoustic instruments. Some tuners clamp onto the guitar's headstock and tune by picking up the strings' vibrations. The tuner will indicate whether the string is in tune, sharp or flat, so all you have to do is adjust the appropriate machine head (tuning peg). If your guitar is way out of tune, an electric tuner may not be able to identify the pitch of the string correctly. If this happens, ask your local music store (or a guitar-playing friend) for help.

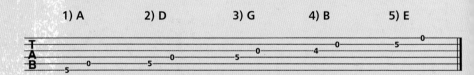

	1) A	2) D	3) G	4) B	5) E

Top tip!

If you're using an electronic tuner, make sure that the guitar's volume is turned up full. When using the tuner's built-in microphone, rest the tuner on your leg, as close to the soundhole as possible.

Pick the string that you're tuning repeatedly but not too quickly. Avoid hitting neighbouring strings because the tuner won't be able to identify the pitch.

On the CD – listen to track 1

To help you get in tune there are some tuning notes on the accompanying CD (see back inside cover) – each string is played three times, starting with the first (high E) string.

Turn the machine head slowly as you play the string – you'll probably only need to move it a fraction of a turn.

Lesson 4
The right-hand position

For fingerpickers, the right hand is where it all happens – so whatever you do don't skip this lesson!

In this lesson you'll be learning how to develop an efficient picking hand technique. Since this book is all about playing fingerstyle guitar this is a crucial lesson, and one you'll probably want to refer back to from time to time. The general rule for fingerpicking is to use the thumb (p) for playing bass notes on the lowest three strings (E, A and D), and the first three fingers (i, m and a) to pick out melody and chord notes on the upper strings (G, B and E). Independence between the thumb and fingers is crucial at every level of fingerstyle guitar playing, so it's important not to hamper finger efficiency with bad hand positioning.

Using thumb- and fingerpicks

There are many different ways to pick the strings with your right hand. Some guitarists use the fleshy part of their fingers; some grow longer fingernails (which can also be artificially enhanced); and some use a combination of fingers and/or thumbpicks. I prefer to use a plastic thumbpick (you can get metal ones too), since it gives the bass notes a little more authority and depth. Although you will see a thumbpick being used in some of the photographs, this doesn't mean that you have to use one too. Experiment to find out which approach works best for you.

Conventional notation

TAB can't tell you which fingers to use to pick the strings; it just tells you which notes to play. Conventional notation is very useful for writing fingerstyle arrangements. Two systems of music are written on one stave, as shown below. The higher notes (stems up) are played with the fingers, the lower notes (stems down) are played with the thumb. The stems-up notes can also be labelled with right-hand fingering as shown here.

Keep your right hand suspended above the strings with the thumb parallel to the bass strings. Your remaining fingers should adopt a clawlike shape above the top three strings. This will enable you to pick the strings without moving your hand.

The side of the thumb always strikes the strings downwards.

Here you can see the thumb with a thumbpick hitting the sixth string. Notice that the angle of the thumb remains the same, whether or not you're using the thumbpick.

Some players lightly "palm mute" the bass strings by resting their palm close to the bridge. This damps the bass notes to prevent them from ringing out too much and drowning the melody.

Top tip!

If you're using a plastic thumbpick and can't get it to fit properly, try immersing it in hot water for a few seconds (but don't hold it with your fingers). It can then easily be moulded to fit your thumb perfectly.

Right-hand finger symbols

Traditional Spanish name abbreviations are used for right-hand fingers – using numbers would create confusion with the fretting hand.

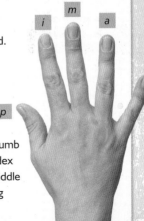

p (*pulgar*) = thumb
i (*indice*) = index
m (*medio*) = middle
a (*anillo*) = ring

Lesson 5
The left-hand position

Don't neglect your left hand – it's important to develop an efficient technique in both hands.

Fingerstyle guitar is about making open chord shapes sound good by using cool picking patterns, isn't it? Well yes, it is up to a point. But if you're struggling to change chords, or muting open strings because you're not fretting the chord shapes properly, then you won't be achieving musical results, however good your picking hand technique is. Developing an efficient left-hand technique is equally important; polished performances will only happen once you can play with maximum economy of movement in both hands. There may well be areas of your left-hand technique that could be improved, so don't skip this lesson.

Left-hand finger numbers

Numbers that appear next to notes in conventional notation indicate a recommended left-hand fingering.

T = thumb
1 = first (index) finger
2 = second (middle) finger
3 = third (ring) finger
4 = fourth (pinky) finger

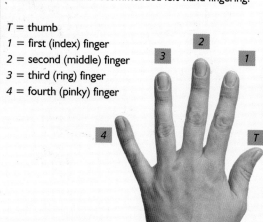

The thumb should be positioned in the centre of the neck. This will provide maximum support for the fingers when you're pressing down on those strings. Be sure to keep your palm off the neck too.

Top tip!
Always try to keep your left-hand thumb positioned in the centre of the neck. Think of this as the default position that you should always return to – even when you use your thumb to fret notes on the sixth string.

Many fingerpickers use the thumb to play bass notes on the sixth string. This is fine, but to avoid straining your hand, make sure you always return to the default position described in step 1.

The tip of your finger should approach the fretboard directly from above and ideally at a 90-degree angle (to avoid damping adjacent strings). It's important to place your finger close to the fret to avoid weak, buzzy-sounding notes.

Aim to keep your fingers hovering above the strings when they're not fretting. This cuts down the movement required and means you will be able to fret notes more easily.

Lesson 6
Playing bass notes

Fingerstyle technique is based on the ability to play an independent bassline, so get your thumb up and running in this lesson.

Unlike the plectrum guitarist who can only play one string at a time, the fingerstyle guitarist can play several strings simultaneously and independently. Playing with your fingers means you can pick out a bassline, hit some accompaniment notes and add a melody on top, all at the same time! Who needs a band?

You'll need to develop a good right-hand thumb technique, since the thumb needs to be able to work independently of the fingers; ultimately it should be able to work in "autopilot" mode. That's why this lesson focuses on basslines and not on melody or chords. You'll learn two simple basslines that don't involve any chord shapes, just fretted and open strings.

Traditionally the thumb (p) plays the notes on the lowest three strings: the sixth string (E), fifth string (A) and fourth string (D). However, there will be occasions when it may stray onto the higher strings, just as the fingers (i, m, a) will sometimes be required to play notes on the lower strings.

Right-hand fingering

Right-hand fingering (i.e., the finger you pluck the string with) is always indicated by Spanish name abbreviations (p, i, m, a). In these examples all of the notes are played with the thumb, indicated by (p) in conjunction with a dashed line.

Repeat bars

A thick line followed by a thin line and two dots is a repeat barline. Always repeat whatever is between repeat barlines (the repeated section can also consist of multiple bars, as in the exercises in this lesson).

Exercise 1
(Listen to track 2)
This riff is played entirely on
the sixth string to allow you
to concentrate on what your
thumb is doing.

*Your thumb should remain parallel to the sixth
string throughout the exercise. Strike the string
with the side of your thumb.*

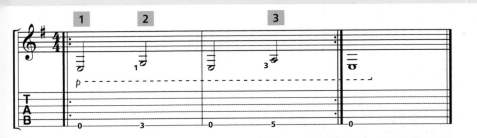

*Your fretting hand should be positioned so that
the first and third fingers will be ready to play
the fretted notes. Here, the first finger plays
the low G on the third fret.*

*Keeping your hand in position, press your
third finger onto the fretboard behind the
fifth fret to play the low A before repeating
the sequence.*

Exercise 2
(Listen to track 3)
This example moves from the sixth
string onto the fifth string, making it
slightly more demanding to play than
exercise 1. Always practise slowly at
first, below the written tempo.

For this exercise, position your hand lower
on the fretboard to allow your third finger
to fret the low G.

Top tip!
Practising with a metronome will
accelerate your rate of progress and help
you develop an accurate sense of time.
Start slowly and build the tempo gradually.

In bar 2, your thumb shifts to the fifth string.
Keep it parallel to the strings.

Keeping your hand in position, use your third
finger to fret the C on the fifth string before
repeating the sequence.

Exercise 3
(Listen to track 4)

Although this example is played at the same tempo, it is based on crotchets (i.e., one note per beat) and so it will feel a lot quicker. Again, begin your practice below the written tempo.

The exercise begins with the side of your thumb striking the sixth string. Keep your thumb parallel to the string.

> **Top tip!**
> Every exercise is demonstrated on the CD. Listen to the example before you begin to play. It's easier to learn something when you know how it should sound.

The low F is played with the first finger of your fretting hand. It's important to fret close behind the fret in order to achieve a clear-sounding note.

At the end of bar 2 your thumb moves onto the fifth string to play the open A note. Strike the string with the side of your thumb.

SEE ALSO

Playing bass notes, page 26

Lesson 7
Adding melody notes

Fingerstyle guitar is all about creating an illusion. It's about fooling the listener into thinking there is more than one guitar playing.

Fingerstyle guitarists achieve this illusion by playing two (or more) melodic lines simultaneously. This may sound complicated but it doesn't have to be; just by adding a few notes to a bassline you can create some beautiful guitar parts, as you'll discover in this lesson. To make the task easier, you'll be using the basslines from lesson 6, so you've already done 50 per cent of the work! This is also the best way to approach any new fingerstyle arrangement; learn the bass pattern first and then figure out how the tune fits around it.

As you work through these three examples you'll also be learning the two principal tools of fingerstyle technique: the "pinch", where a

melody note is played simultaneously with a bass note, and "syncopated" picking, where a melody note is played between bass notes. The pinch is the simpler of the techniques: as the thumb strikes a bass note, a finger simultaneously picks a melody note on one of the higher strings. Syncopation occurs when notes are played in the gaps (i.e., the off beats) between bass notes. It's the combination of these two concepts that makes a good fingerstyle pattern sound cool.

Counting the beats

| 1 | and | 2 | and | 3 | and | 4 | and |

When you're playing off-beat notes you'll need to add the word "and" after the number of each beat. Counting "and" between the beats will enable you to accurately play the awkward notes that fall in the gaps.

Exercise 1
(Listen to track 5)

This first example is a pinching workout to allow you to get used to using your thumb and fingers simultaneously. Keep your fingers hovering over their respective strings even when they're not picking.

While striking the sixth string with your thumb, your second finger (m) simultaneously picks the second string.

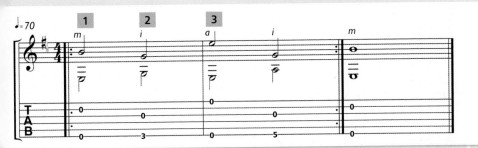

The second pinch should be played with your thumb and first finger (i).

This pinch is played with your thumb striking the sixth string while your third finger (a) simultaneously picks the first string.

Exercise 2
(Listen to track 6)

This example introduces syncopation
by adding melody notes in the first bar
and picking out sustained chord notes
in the second.

Top tip!

If you're getting frustrated, take a break
and try again later at a slower tempo.
Once you can play something three times
without mistakes, you've nailed it!

*This exercise opens with a thumb and second
finger (m) pinch. Notice how the remaining
fingers remain above their respective strings.
The "let ring" instruction requires you to keep
your first finger in position to allow the chord
notes to ring into each other.*

*The thumb is ready to strike the sixth string
after the second finger (m) has picked the D
on the second string.*

*After striking the open fifth string with your
thumb, pick the third string with your first
finger (i).*

Exercise 3
(Listen to track 7)

In this example pinched and syncopated notes are mixed to create an exciting picking pattern. The second bar is quite tricky, so practise it well below tempo (start around 55 bpm).

> **Top tip!**
> Listen to the CD. It's also good practice to read through the music as you're listening. Focus on the upper stave – this will explain the rhythmic content of each exercise.

The opening pinch of this example is played with your thumb and third finger (a). Keeping your thumb parallel to the string will make this busy bassline easier to play.

Fret the high D on the second string with your fourth finger. Your second finger simultaneously frets the low F♯ on the sixth string.

The thumb and first finger (i) should be positioned close together for the pinch on the third beat of bar 2.

Lesson 8
Open chord shapes

A thorough understanding of the basic open chord shapes is essential for playing fingerstyle – check you're up to speed in this lesson.

Even if you feel confident about your chord vocabulary, it's well worth taking the time to check out the shapes in this lesson. There are bound to be some you haven't used before or alternative fingerings you haven't considered.

This isn't intended to be a music theory book, but a basic understanding of harmony is highly desirable; it will help you make informed musical decisions when you're creating arrangements of your own. So let's briefly talk about the theory behind chords. Chords can essentially be grouped into three families: major, minor and dominant sevenths. (If this is all new to you it's probably worth getting your hands on a good music theory book for reference.) As a basic rule of thumb, major chords sound happy, minor chords sad, and the dominant seventh chord sounds unsettled (i.e., not at rest). The dominant seventh is an extremely important

chord since it creates tension and motion; it naturally wants to resolve to a chord a perfect fourth above (the perfect cadence – a musical equivalent of a full stop). It's the tritone (flattened fifth) in the dominant seventh that creates this harmonic unrest. This dissonant interval was outlawed in the Middle Ages since it was believed to be capable of summoning the devil; hence the term "the devil's music" for the blues, which is based entirely on dominant seventh chords.

Chord formula

Major chord = R - 3 - 5
Minor chord = R - ♭3 - 5
Dominant seventh = R - 3 - 5 - ♭7

Basic chord theory

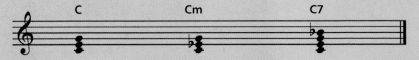

Major and minor chords contain just three notes: a root note (that the chord takes its name from), a third and a fifth. These are called "triads". By stacking an extra note on top of the major triad, a four-note dominant seventh is created. Understanding the way chords are constructed gives you more options; it also allows you to use notes other than the root in the bass (these are called "inversions").

Example 1
Basic major shapes

There are five basic open major shapes (not including inversions). Fingering is indicated next to the relevant finger dot. Only commonly used inversions are given.

C

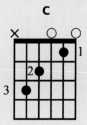

C/G

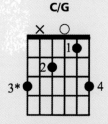

A

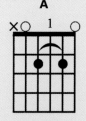

G

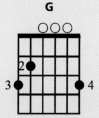

E

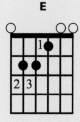

D

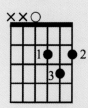

D/F#

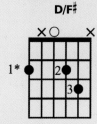

* Bass notes on the sixth string can also be played with the thumb.

Top tip!

When a chord has a note other than its root in the bass it is called an "inversion". Inversions are indicated by a slash chord symbol like the one below. The left-hand symbol is the chord, the right-hand symbol the bass note.

C/G = C chord with G in bass

Example 2
Basic minor shapes

Since there are no open shapes for C minor or G minor, there are only three basic open minor shapes. Once again, only commonly used inversions are given.

A/m	Am/G	Em
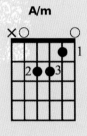	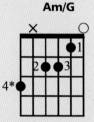	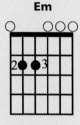

Dm	Dm/F	Dm/C
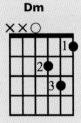	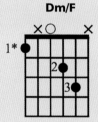	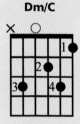

* Bass notes on the sixth string can also be played with the thumb.

Top tip!
Chord symbols are always abbreviated in guitar music. Here are the most common ones:

Chord	Symbol
C major	C
C minor	Cm or Cmin
C dominant seventh	C7

Example 3
Basic dominant seventh shapes

With five basic open shapes, plus three commonly used inversions, there are eight dominant seventh shapes to learn. As with all of the chords in this lesson, it's not always necessary to fret every note – it all depends on how many strings you're picking with your right hand.

C7

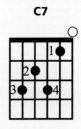

C7/G

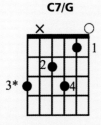

A7

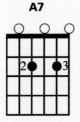

G7

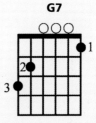

G7/B

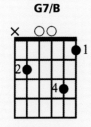

D7

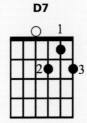

D7/F#

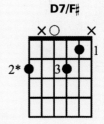

E7

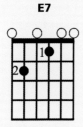

Lesson 9
Three easy pieces

Three easy accompaniments that will teach you the secrets of the great singer-songwriters.

When fingerpicking technique is applied to a simple chord sequence it suddenly comes alive, sounding much cooler than it would with a boring old strumming pattern. All the great singer-songwriters understood this, from Paul Simon to James Taylor, Joni Mitchell to Eva Cassidy. All you need is a simple pattern that can be repeated through a chord sequence, and you've got everything you need to create classy accompaniments. By varying the attack of the picking hand, dynamics and contrast between verses or choruses can be achieved

without even changing the pattern. The original picking patterns were adapted from the banjo accompaniments of bluegrass music that came out of the Kentucky Mountains during the 1920s and 1930s. But it was the American folk revival of the late 1950s and early 1960s that gave birth to the new singer-songwriter genre, and defined the art of fingerpicked accompaniments. Pioneering artists such as Bob Dylan, Joan Baez, Pete Seeger and Arlo Guthrie all cut their teeth on the bohemian coffee bar circuit of Greenwich Village, New York City.

Arpeggiated chords

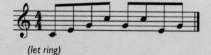

(let ring)

let ring - - - - - - - - - - - - - - - - - - -

Picking patterns could easily be mistaken for a sequence of arpeggios. Always look out for the "let ring" instruction, which indicates that it's actually an arpeggiated chord. Simply hold down the chord shape and pick out the notes as indicated. In the first example, the "let ring" instruction appears in parentheses at the beginning of the piece, indicating that the whole arrangement should be played this way. In the second example, the "let ring" instruction is followed by a dashed line, indicating that only a specific section should be played this way.

The chords you'll need for this lesson:

C	Am	C7	A7	D7	G7

Exercise 1
(Listen to track 8)

This example is typical of the singer-songwriter style of accompaniment that became popular in the 1960s. It's a straightforward one-bar pattern that also makes an ideal warm-up exercise for your right hand.

The example opens with a pinch on the first and fifth strings; strike the bass note with your thumb while simultaneously picking the first string with your third finger (a).

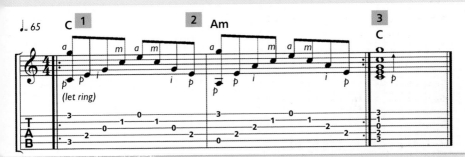

Don't forget that your thumb should play all the notes on the fourth string. Here, you can see the thumb playing the last note in bar 1.

To play the concluding chord, simply brush your thumb across the strings, strike the fifth string first and ascend to the first string with a sweeping motion.

Exercise 2
(Listen to track 9)

This fingerpicking workout will help familiarize you with the basic open dominant seventh shapes. It's based on a cycle of fifths sequence that pulls back to the tonic chord, C7. Musicians call sequences like this a "turnaround".

The C7 chord is the same as a regular C chord but with your fourth finger fretting the extra note on the third string.

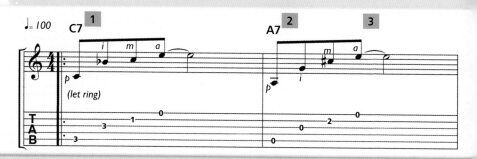

The thumb is ready to strike the fifth string while the remaining fingers (i, m and a) are correctly poised over the treble strings.

Keep your fretting hand in position while your third finger (a) picks the open first string.

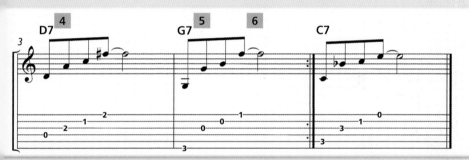

The bass note (open D) of the D7 chord is played with your thumb. The remaining fretting hand fingers are allocated to the treble strings as before.

Top tip!
You don't always have to take all your fingers off the strings when you change chords. Check to see if any notes repeat in the following chord – you can then leave those fingers in place for a smoother, easier chord change.

There's no need to fret the full G7 chord, as the fifth string is not sounded. Just use your first and third fingers to fret the outermost strings.

The last note of the G7 chord (F) is picked with your third finger (a). Notice how the thumb simultaneously hovers above the fifth string ready to play the next bass note.

Exercise 3
(Listen to track 10)

A classic minor sequence that uses chord inversions to create a hypnotic descending bassline. This kind of sequence was popularized during the 1960s and features in many classic songs of the era such as The Beatles' "Dear Prudence" and Led Zeppelin's "Babe I'm Gonna Leave You".

This photograph illustrates the correct D minor fingering for this example. The fourth finger frets the second string while the third hovers above the fifth ready for the following chord.

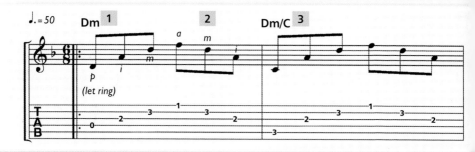

Keep your thumb hovering above the fifth string while picking out the melody notes. Here, you can see the second finger (m) picking the second string with the thumb in position.

By fretting the second string with your fourth finger, your third finger remains free to fret the low C at the start of bar 2.

Although you're probably used to playing G chord bass notes on the sixth string, this chord inversion's lowest note is on the fifth. Play it with your thumb.

Top tip!
Don't be put off by that odd-looking time signature in this example – 6/8 is very common in fingerpicking accompaniments, especially in folk music. It's called "compound time" because unlike 4/4 (or "common time") you can count two pulses: six quavers or two dotted crotchets (that's why the quavers are grouped into threes).

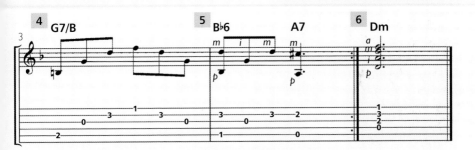

Play the pinch at the start of bar 3 with your thumb and second finger.

All of the notes of the final D minor chord should be picked simultaneously, using your thumb and fingers.

Lesson 10
Syncopated patterns

Playing chord notes between bass notes creates interesting rhythms and cool picking patterns.

If you want to create more interesting picking patterns, there's no better way to do it than by playing your chord and melody notes "in the gaps" between bass notes. The musical term for this is "syncopation" and it's what gives all music, not just fingerstyle guitar, rhythm and groove. The ability to play syncopated patterns with your fingers (i, m and a) while the thumb (p) maintains a constant rhythm is a prerequisite of fingerstyle guitar technique. Normally,

syncopation is achieved by a combination of instruments playing against each other in an ensemble setting; the fingerstyle guitarist creates syncopation by playing notes against a bassline played with the thumb. So it's extremely important to nail the rhythmic content of the examples in this lesson. In all three examples the thumb plays notes on the beat, with the fingers adding notes on off beats. This is how that all-important syncopation is created.

Grace notes and slurs

Hammer-on/pull-off played rhythmically

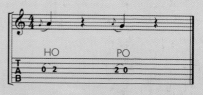

Hammer-on/pull-off using grace notes

Ornamentation makes guitar parts sound professional. Guitarists use it to create an individual and identifiable sound of their own. There are many types of ornamentation, but it's the slur you are focusing on here. A slur is played on guitar by "hammering on" or "pulling off" to a note on the same string. Only the first note is picked; the second is created by hammering the finger onto the string, or pulling it off with a sideways, flicking motion. Slurs can be played rhythmically (see the first example), or as "squashed in" (grace) notes (as shown in the second example).

The chords you'll need for this lesson:

C

G7

G

G/F# 3fr.

Em

Em/D

Exercise 1
(Listen to track 11)

In this example a melodic bassline is played against a repeated pedal note on the third string. Practise the bassline separately before adding the pedal note on the off beats.

Although a C chord is given above the bar, it's much easier to play this example when the full shape isn't fretted. Here, only the opening C bass note is fretted with the third finger.

Keep your second finger in position behind the second fret while playing the F with your third finger. That way it will already be in position for the next note.

Your first finger (i) repeatedly strikes the open third strings after each bass note is sounded.

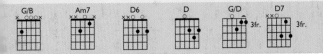

Exercise 2
(Listen to track 12)

Another 6/8 pattern, this time providing a workout for the first (i) and second (m) fingers of the right hand. Add the hammer-ons (bars 1 and 4) only when you can play the example confidently.

The fretting hand is shown in position at the start of bar 1. Use your third finger for the G on the fifth fret, and your first for the high D on the second fret.

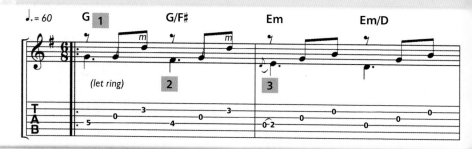

While your thumb strikes the fourth string, your remaining fretting hand fingers should be in position above their respective strings.

To play the hammer-on at the start of bar 2, pick the open fourth string and fret the E firmly with your second finger.

4

> **Top tip!**
> Don't forget that it's not always necessary to fret all of the notes in a chord shape. Take, for instance, the final G chord in this exercise – only the root note on the sixth string is fretted because the fifth and first strings aren't picked.

Only the third and first fingers are used to fret the C chord. Since the fourth string is not sounded, the second finger can remain in position above the string.

5

It's not necessary to fret all of the notes of the G/B chord. Just fret the fifth string with your second finger.

6

The concluding G chord is simultaneously picked by all the fingers of your fretting hand.

Exercise 3
(Listen to track 13)

This last example uses all three of
the right-hand fingers (i, m and a).
The technique of moving three-note
chords against an open D pedal note
has created many cool riffs including
The Who's "Pinball Wizard" and the
Kings of Leon's "The Bucket".

*Use your first finger to play the opening
hammer-on in the pick-up bar. This leaves your
second finger free for the A on the third string
that quickly follows.*

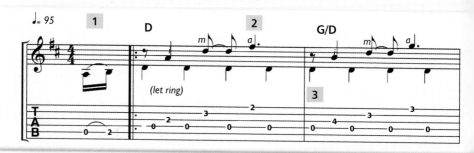

*While picking the first string with your third
finger (a), your thumb should remain in position
for the next bass note.*

*Fret all three notes of the G/D chord
simultaneously. This allows all the notes to
ring clearly for the full bar.*

Fret the C on the fifth fret with your third finger. The full D7 shape ideally should be formed at the same time.

Top tip!
Practise each part separately before playing them together. This is especially important when you're playing syncopated notes against a bassline. Remember that stems-down notes are played with the thumb (p), while stems-up notes are played with the fingers (i, m and a).

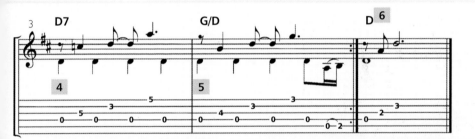

At the start of bar 4, the thumb strikes the fourth string. Notice how the remaining fingers are also in position above the treble strings.

The final D chord has no third and so can be fretted using only your first and third fingers.

SEE ALSO
Transposing patterns, page 54

Lesson II
Moveable chord shapes

With moveable chord shapes you can play any chord in any key. This lesson teaches you the essential shapes.

There are two types of moveable chord shapes: barre chords spanning five or six strings and smaller four-note chords. All moveable shapes are based on some form of open chord: barre chords are based on the open E and A shapes. If an E chord is played a fret higher with the same open strings ringing, it's no longer a plain old E major chord but the exotically named E(♭9,♭13)sus4. This distinctively Spanish-sounding chord is often referred to as the "Phrygian chord" since it conjures up the sound of the mode. The Phrygian chord is perfect when you need to inject Spanish flavours into your music, but it's not a moveable shape as such. However, if you move the open strings with the E shape by pressing your finger flat across the first fret (you'll need to change the E fingering to free

up your first finger), then voilà! You'll have an F major chord that becomes F♯ on the second fret and G on the third, etc. Moveable minor or dominant chords can be achieved in the same way. In fact there are many more possibilities – pretty much any open E shape can be adapted to work as a barre chord. This principle can also be applied to the open A chord, except the sixth string has to be damped since the root note of the chord is on the fifth.

The moveable four-note shapes that you will be looking at in this lesson are based on the upper four notes of a full six-string barre chord. The chords derived from this shape are lighter sounding and very useful for playing four-string picking patterns with, particularly when using the D chord, as you'll see in the next lesson.

Right-hand fingering

barre chord ⟶ open chord

The evolution of the moveable six-string barre chord is illustrated here. If you've never played barre chords before, you will find them a little difficult at first. Be patient and practise them frequently to build up strength in your hand.

Example 1
Six-string barre chords

These are shown as F chords, but transposition is achieved by simply moving the shape along the neck. Two shapes are given for Fm7 and F7; the second shape in each case has the minor seventh interval doubled an octave higher to enhance the "seventh" quality of the chord.

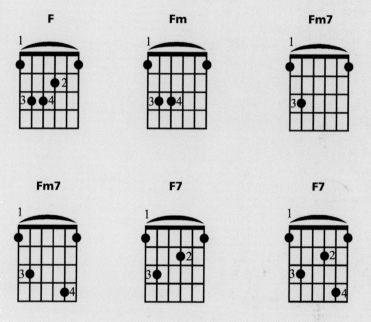

Example 2
Five-string barre chords

Once again, the shapes are illustrated in their lowest possible position on the first fret (i.e., B♭). As with the six-string shapes, two voicings for B♭m7 and B♭7 are given, the second with the minor seventh interval voiced an octave higher.

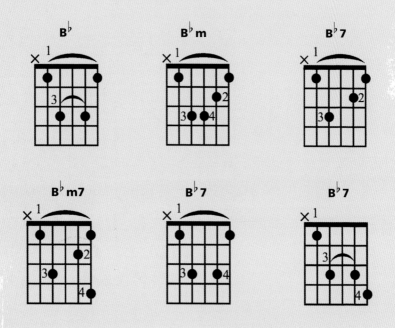

Top tip!

Finding five- and six-string barre chords quickly is dependent on a thorough knowledge of the notes on the fifth and sixth strings. You'll find it helpful to learn the notes in pairs, i.e., on the fifth fret the notes will be A (sixth string) and D (fifth string), since this is often how they occur in a progression.

Example 3
Moveable four-string shapes

These voicings are derived from the upper notes of the full six-string barre chord. They are ideal when a lighter, less dense voicing is required and work well with open D shapes. It's also an easy shape for adding intervals such as the sus4 and add9.

Fadd9

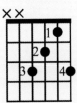

F

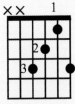

Fsus4

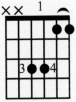

F6

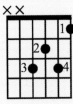

Fm

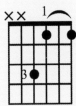

Fm7

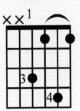

F7

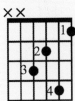

F°

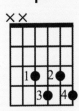

Top tip!

Always try to relate new shapes to those you already know. For instance, the full F barre chord is simply the open E shape moved up one fret and barred. This not only makes the shapes easier to learn, but will also help you create any chord voicing you need by adapting one of the five basic open shapes: C, A, G, E and D.

Lesson 12
Transposing patterns

Here you will learn how to adapt picking patterns to fit four-string, five-string or six-string chord shapes.

Chord shapes generally fall into one of three groups: those with their root note on the sixth string, the fifth string or the fourth string (the chords G, C and D are good examples of these respective string groups). The lower the bass note, the greater the number of strings above it. For example, the lowest note of an E chord is the open sixth string, leaving five strings above it for creating a picking pattern.

Only three strings are available above the open fourth string (the root note) of a D chord.

So a picking pattern that works well on a G chord often needs modification before it will work with a C or a D chord. Sometimes this is just a simple matter of picking the bass note on a different string, but what if you've got a cool picking pattern for Am that uses all five strings and your next chord is D? Sometimes the original pattern just needs a little rethinking to solve the problem. In this lesson you'll be exploring some of the options and melodic tools used to transpose picking patterns.

Contrary motion

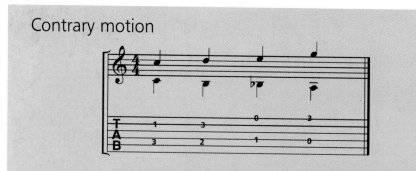

This is the musical term that describes two melodic lines moving in opposite directions. It's an established melodic tool that sounds great in fingerstyle patterns. It's usually applied to the bass note and the highest voice of the melody/chord but can also work with "inner" voices too. In the example shown you can see a descending bassline played against a simultaneously rising melody.

The chords you'll need for this lesson:

C   D   G7/B   Am7   F   G

Exercise 1
(Listen to track 14)

Here the picking pattern for the C chord spans the middle four strings. The pattern is transposed to a D chord by simply shifting the entire pattern across the strings. This is the simplest method, but not always the answer when more interesting voice leading is required.

Because the picking hand fingers are playing the inner four strings, the opening pinch should be picked with your thumb and third finger (a).

Pick the fourth string at the end of bar 1 with your first finger.

In the second bar the picking hand fingers span the top four strings. The first pinch should be picked with your thumb and third finger (a).

Am   C/G

Exercise 2
(Listen to track 15)

Here the right-hand fingers (i, m and a) play the top three strings throughout, allowing the thumb to play bass notes on any of the lower strings without having to change the pattern at all. Notice the contrary motion in the first two bars.

Use your thumb to strike the fifth string while your third finger (a) picks the open first string.

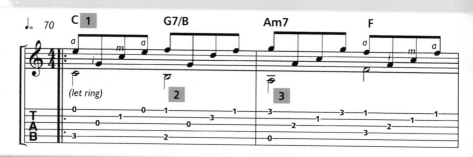

In this example, the first string of the G7/B chord is picked, so fret the chord with your first and second fingers.

This unusual Am7 voicing does not include the fourth string but adds a high G on the first string. Fret the chord with your first, second and fourth fingers.

This G chord includes the open first string (E) on the pinch, so you only need to fret the sixth string with your third finger.

Top tip!
Where possible, try to allow notes to ring into the following bar. For instance, in this exercise the open G note should be allowed to ring continuously throughout the last bars.

Add the D on the second string with your third finger. Keep your third finger in position to allow the bass note to ring for its full value.

Your first finger (i) should pick the open third string throughout bar 4, as illustrated.

Exercise 3

(Listen to track 16)

Finally, the two previous concepts are mixed: a bassline starting on the fifth string descends to the sixth while the finger notes (p, i, m and a) remain on the fourth, third and second strings respectively. In bars 3 and 4 the entire pattern is shifted across the strings for the D and F chords.

In bars 1 and 2 your picking fingers shift across the strings so that your first finger (i) picks the fourth string.

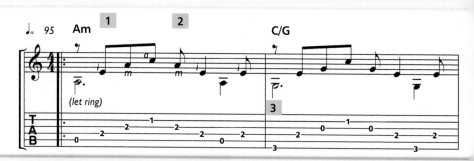

Pick the A on the third string with your second finger (m). Keep your picking fingers (i, m and a) in position above their respective strings.

At the start of bar 2 the thumb moves onto the sixth string. Keep your fingers in position ready to pick out the melody notes.

In bars 3 and 4 your picking fingers shift back across the strings so that your thumb now strikes the fourth string.

Top tip!
Before transposing a picking pattern, make sure you understand it in its original form. This will avoid inadvertently changing the pattern and making the process unnecessarily confusing.

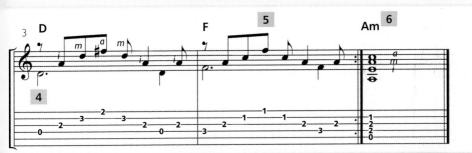

Pick the high F on the first string with your third finger (a). The thumb should remain in position, ready to replay the fourth string.

The notes of the final Am chord are picked simultaneously using all your picking fingers. Notice how the first three fingers (i, m and a) have returned to the lower set of strings.

Lesson 13
Semiquaver patterns

Learn how to play semiquaver patterns and keep your music grooving at slower tempos.

So far you have only played picking patterns constructed from quavers. In other words, the only subdivision you've had to make is to halve the beat, i.e., when notes fall on the second half of the beat (the offbeat). If you're tapping your foot when you play (and you should be!), the off-beat quavers occur when your foot is up and the downbeats when your foot is down.

Semiquavers are a little trickier; now each quaver is halved to create four subdivisions per beat. This sounds complicated, but once you become familiar with the sound of

semiquavers and how to count them correctly, they shouldn't be a problem. You've probably played semiquaver rhythms before without even realizing it! The point of semiquavers is not to be able to challenge your mate to a fingerpicking shred-off, duelling banjos-style (some players might disagree), but to play more interesting accompaniments at slower tempos. Classic examples of semiquaver picking patterns can be heard in Simon and Garfunkel's "The Boxer" or the Eagles' "Hotel California".

Counting semiquavers

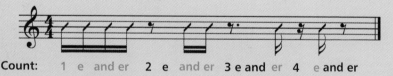

Count: 1 e and er   2 e and er 3 e and er 4   e and er

When you're learning a new semiquaver picking pattern it's a good idea to play it slowly and tap your foot in quavers (i.e., twice as fast as you normally would). Ultimately, however, you'll need to be able to relate it to a regular crotchet note pulse. This example illustrates the accepted counting method (the greyed highlights indicate where the notes fall) that adds "e" and "er" to a regular quaver count.

The chords you'll need for this lesson:

D5	D5/C	G/B	C	Am	Dm7

Exercise 1
(Listen to track 17)

This example creates contrast by using a syncopated semiquaver pattern against a simple descending bassline. The repeated semiquaver rhythm is simple but effective; the first low A note falls on "1 and" while the second is slightly earlier on "2 e".

Fret the D5 chord using your first and third fingers. This will leave your second finger free to play the C bass note in bar 2.

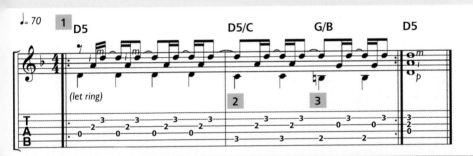

Keeping your first and third fingers in position, move your second finger onto the third fret of the fifth string.

To fret the G/B chord, simply move your first finger onto the fifth string while keeping your third finger in position.

Dm7/G

C/G

D7/F♯

D/F♯

G

G7

Exercise 2
(Listen to track 18)
This is a great warm-up exercise for getting all your picking fingers going. The chord notes are played on the top three strings with the fingers (i, m and a) throughout.

Because the fourth string of the C chord is not picked, you don't have to fret it. Here, you can see the chord being played with just the first and third fingers.

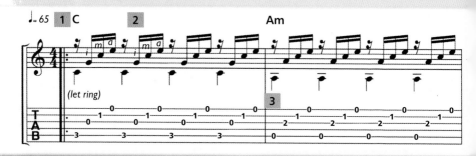

As you pick the third string with your first finger (i), your second and third fingers (m and a) should be in position above the strings.

Since the fourth string is not sounded, you can fret the Am chord with just your first and second fingers. This also facilitates a quick change to the Dm7 in the following bar.

Before you pick the first note of the chord, make sure all your fingers are in position above their respective strings.

Top tip!

In the first example you probably noticed the chord symbol D5. This indicates a "power chord", which is more commonly used by rock guitarists because it sounds great with distortion. A power chord is harmonically ambiguous since it has no third, i.e., it is neither major nor minor.

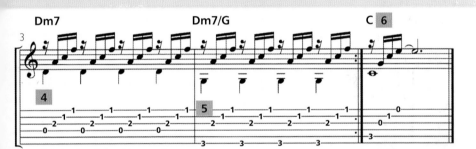

Keep your three picking hand fingers in position as your thumb moves across the strings to fret the low G bass note.

The concluding C chord is played with the original picking sequence, i.e., thumb on the fifth string and fingers (i, m and a) on the top three strings.

Exercise 3
(Listen to track 19)
Using semiquaver patterns against a
6/8 pulse can create beautifully
hypnotic accompaniments like this
one. It's essential to maintain a steady,
rhythmic picking pattern throughout.

*In this example your picking hand fingers shift
across the strings. This step demonstrates the
correct positioning with the fingers (i, m and a)
above the fourth, third and second strings.*

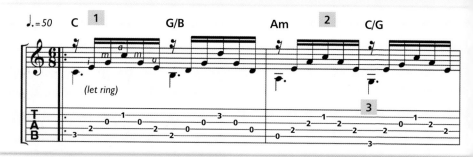

*With the picking hand fingers shifted across the
strings, your third finger (a) plays the second
string in this example.*

*Without disrupting the position of your picking
fingers, move your thumb across the strings to
play the G bass note in bar 2.*

To fret the F♯ bass note correctly, the thumb reaches around the top of the guitar neck.

Top tip!
To create more dramatic endings, musicians often pull back the tempo before the final chord. The musical term for this is "rallentando". It's usually abbreviated and written below the main stave at the point where you should slow down, as in bar 4 of this example.

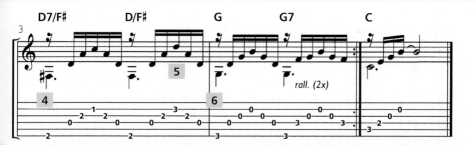

Use your fourth finger to fret the D on the third fret, keeping your thumb in position.

Since the first and fifth strings are not sounded, the G chord in bar 4 can be fretted with just your third finger.

Lesson 14
Barre chord patterns

Transform your electric guitar technique – try some barre chord riffs that sound cool played fingerstyle.

Fingerstyle technique is not the sole preserve of acoustic guitarists; it's great for electric players too. Picking out a rhythmic pattern with your fingers transforms a predictable chord sequence into something more sophisticated. It's a cool way to play ballads and slower grooves, too, particularly if you're in a band without keyboards.

However, as electric guitars amplify every nuance of your playing, fingerpicked open chords can sometimes sound a little messy. Because barre chords contain no open strings, they are less resonant and can be muted by simply releasing the pressure of

your fretting hand. This is why many electric guitarists prefer these shapes for fingerpicking. They can be a little awkward when you need to change chords quickly, and it's a sackable offence to pause between changes when you're playing with other musicians! So, to speed up your barre chord changes, always move your fingers as little as possible; ideally they should remain in contact with the strings at all times. By releasing the pressure of your fretting hand (without taking the fingers off the strings), you'll find that you can just slide the shape along the strings and make a much quicker change of chords.

The chords you'll need for this lesson:

Exercise 1
(Listen to track 20)

This semiquaver picking pattern is ideal for ballads and slower rock grooves. Only the melody notes on the first and third beats coincide with a bass note (a pinch); the remaining notes are syncopated. This picking pattern wouldn't sound out of place in a Red Hot Chili Peppers' tune, so it's ideal for funk rock styles.

The Em chord should be fretted with your second finger (m) hovering above the eighth fret. As you play the opening pinch, hammer your second finger onto the string.

The thumb plays an alternating bassline throughout. This photograph demonstrates the correct positioning of the picking fingers with the thumb playing the fifth string.

The opening pinch in bar 2 should be played with your thumb and second finger (m).

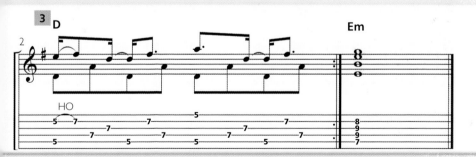

E   D/E   Dsus4   C/D   G/C   Bsus4

Exercise 2
(Listen to track 21)

This easy picking pattern uses only the first two fingers (i, m) and thumb (p) of your picking hand. The highest melody note (E) is repeated throughout the first three bars. This is called a "pedal note". The inclusion of the non-diatonic chord C (i.e., not belonging to the key of E) makes this example reminiscent of Radiohead's work.

Fret the full six-string barre chord shape with your first finger snugly behind (not on) the fifth fret.

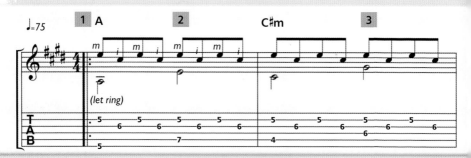

On the third beat your thumb moves onto the fifth string to play the pinch, with your second finger (m) picking the second string.

This pinch is played with your thumb striking the fourth string while your second finger (m) simultaneously picks the second string.

You'll find the C chord much easier to play when you barre across the strings with your third finger.

Top tip!
Playing major barre chords with a root on the fifth string is easier when you play the upper notes with a barre. Don't barre with your first finger (this only needs to fret the bass note) instead flatten your third finger across the second, third and fourth strings.

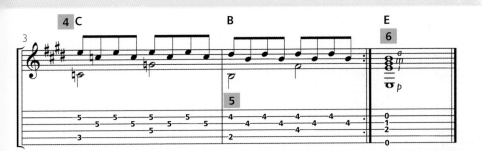

Keeping the C chord shape intact, simply slide it down the strings to the second fret for the B chord that follows.

The concluding E chord should be picked using all your fingers simultaneously.

Exercise 3
(Listen to track 22)

Instead of picking individual notes, the three picking hand fingers (i, m and a) pick three chord notes simultaneously in this example. This creates a much funkier style of accompaniment suitable for many genres.

Pick the upper notes of the chord using all three of your picking hand fingers (i, m and a) simultaneously.

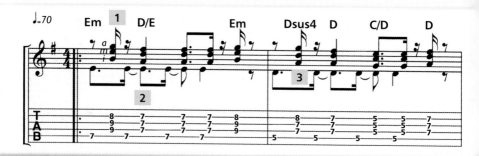

The D/E chord is played with your first finger barring across the seventh fret. The unused fingers should remain hovering above their respective frets.

Fret the D chord by barring across the fifth fret. The "sus4" can then be added with your fourth finger.

Top tip!

Remember that it's easier to learn tricky picking patterns when you break them down into two parts: melody (stems up) and bass notes (stems down). Always learn parts separately before you put them together.

As you pick the bass note with your thumb, your remaining fingers should already be in position above their respective strings, ready to pick the chord notes.

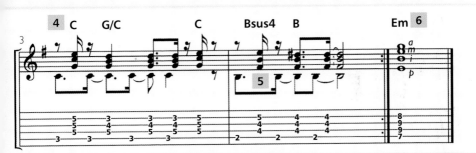

As soon as your thumb has picked the bass note, your fingers pick out the remaining chord notes simultaneously.

Pick all four notes of the concluding Em chord simultaneously, using your thumb and fingers together.

SEE ALSO Three easy pieces, page 38; Transposing patterns, page 54; Country workout, page 78

Lesson 15
Roots and fifths

Learn how to create driving basslines using the root and fifth of each chord.

The fingerpicking patterns up until now have contained only simple basslines, since you've been concentrating on developing interesting rhythms and arpeggio patterns with the right hand. Now it's time to turn your attention to the thumb once again and max up the bass notes! Keeping a driving bass pattern going with the thumb doesn't just sound more interesting, it also frees up your fingers to play more melodically, as you will see in the next lesson.

Start by creating basslines using two intervals that can be found in every chord: the root

and the fifth. The root note, as you've already discovered, is usually the lowest note of a chord (unless the chord is an inversion). The fifth interval (usually a perfect fifth but sometimes diminished or augmented) is often (but not always) the note above the root in many chord shapes. Sometimes it's two strings above, as in the chords C and G. To find the fifth of a chord, just count up five letter names (including the root). So the fifth of a C major chord is C + four letter names = G. You can then easily identify the fifth in any chord that you're playing.

Finding the fifth of a chord

The fifth of a chord is often, but not always, the note above the root. In this example, counting up five letter names (including the root) reveals G to be the fifth of a C major chord. You can then identify the note within the chord. When the chord's root note is on the fifth string (e.g. C), you can also add the fifth below the chord. For a C chord, this would be a G on the third fret of the sixth string.

The chords you'll need for this lesson:

C D G C7 A7 D7

Exercise 1
(Listen to track 23)

This is a reworking of exercise 1 from lesson 12. Adding a root and fifth bassline heightens the groove by creating syncopation on the third beat. Notice that the root note always precedes the fifth in the bass.

Because your first finger (i) will be picking notes on the fourth string, your third finger (a) plays the high note in this pinch.

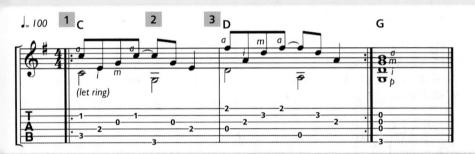

To play the G bass note, simply move your third finger across to the sixth string. Keep your remaining fingers in position.

In bar 2 your picking hand moves across the strings so that your thumb and third finger (a) play the first pinch.

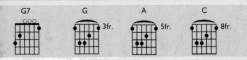

Exercise 2
(Listen to track 24)

You've seen this pattern before, too. It appeared in exercise 2 in lesson 9, but in a much simpler form. Doubling up the arpeggiated pattern played with the fingers, and adding a root and fifth bassline transforms it into a more exciting accompaniment.

Pick the first bass note of the root and fifth accompaniment with your thumb on the fifth string. Notice that the remaining fingers are already in position above the strings.

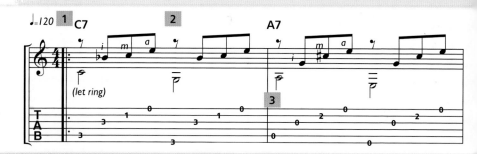

Move your third finger across the strings to fret the G bass note while keeping your remaining fingers on the frets.

As you play the first note of bar 2 with your thumb, your fingers should be in position above the top three strings.

Move your thumb onto the fifth string to play the second note of the root and fifth bassline in bar 3.

Top tip!
Allowing root and fifth bass notes to ring into each other sounds messy and spoils the bassline. By resting the fleshy part of your palm on the bridge you can lightly damp the lower strings. This improves the dynamic of the bass part and allows the melody to ring clearly.

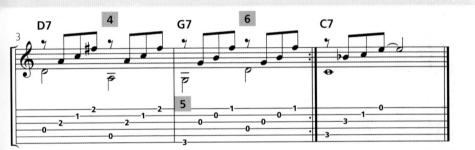

Since the fifth string is not sounded, the G7 chord can be fretted using only your first and third fingers.

To play the second bass note in bar 4, skip over the fifth string and onto the fourth. Use your picking fingers to repeat the same pattern as before.

Exercise 3
(Listen to track 25)

Barre chords are ideal for creating root and fifth picking patterns, especially when the same chord shape is moved along the neck. This allows the picking pattern to remain constant, ideal when playing at quicker tempos.

Fret the G chord by barring across the third fret with your first finger. To ensure all of the notes ring clearly, place your finger just behind the fret, not on top of it.

Here you can see the thumb picking the second note of the root and fifth bassline, while the first finger (i) is poised to pick the melody on the third string.

The opening pinch of bar 2 should be played with your thumb and second finger (m).

As you move the barre chord shape up the neck, you'll find it more difficult to place the third and fourth fingers behind the same fret. Tuck the fourth finger just under the third.

Top tip!

In this exercise you may have noticed the 2/2 time signature at the start of the piece. This is referred to as "cut common" (since 4/4 is common time) or "cut time". When the tempo increases it is easier to count fewer beats per bar. In this case, you're counting two beats per bar (minims).

Release the chord shape and lift your fingers off the frets to allow the open E string to be sounded on beat 2.

Fret the ascending bassline with your first finger. This allows the full barre chord shape to remain intact (but hovering above the strings) as you slide, ready for a quick return to the G.

Lesson 16
Country workout

Now that you can play root and fifth basslines this original country tune will let you show off your skills!

In lesson 15 you learned how to identify, locate and play the perfect fifth interval; you also discovered that it could be used to create driving basslines. In this lesson you'll be using root and fifth basslines in your first fingerpicking arrangement, an original tune with a strong country flavour.

By breaking arrangements into shorter, more manageable sections, you'll find them easier and more fun to learn. Give yourself plenty of time to absorb new material; with regular practice and a methodical approach nothing will be beyond your reach. Don't forget that it's important to understand how the bass notes (played with the thumb) and the melody notes (played with the fingers) interact with each other. Before playing them together, play each part separately to identify which melody notes are pinched and which are syncopated.

Pick-up measures

count 1 2   3   4

Sometimes a tune will start before the first full bar of music. This is called a "pick-up bar", and it means the tune starts partway through the count in. It's not necessary for the pick-up bar to equal a full measure (in this example it's just two beats long), so it's usually only as long as the notes contained within it. A pick-up bar is always followed by a double barline to indicate the start of the first full bar of the tune.

**The chords you'll
need for this lesson:**

G

C

D7/F#

D/F#

C/G

Virtuoso country fingerpicker
Brad Paisley demonstrates how
to pick out a mean bassline and
look cool at the same time!

Exercise
(Listen to track 26)

The pinch at the beginning of bar 1 should be played with your thumb and second finger (m).

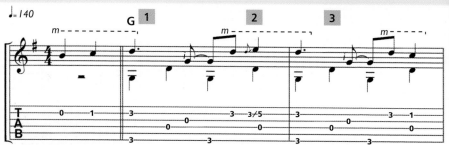

As soon as you've played the D on the second string, slide your finger up to the fifth fret. Don't re-pick the string; the movement of your finger will create the new note.

Here, you can see the thumb striking the fourth string. Remember that your thumb will be playing a constant alternating bass pattern throughout the piece.

Leave your third finger in position (on the low G) while you fret the A on the third string with your second finger.

Top tip!

Remember to lightly damp the bass notes. This prevents them from ringing into each other and sounding messy. Rest the palm of your hand just on the bridge and allow the palm to lightly touch the lower strings. This will create a more percussive, rhythmic bassline, and also allow the listener to hear the melody clearly.

Play the fifth string bass notes with your thumb. Notice how the fingers remain in position above their respective strings.

The opening pinch in this bar should be played with your thumb and second finger (m).

Keep the C chord shape intact as shown, adding the D on the second string with your fourth finger.

By flattening your second finger (m) across the third string you can easily add the A note to the C chord.

Here, the thumb is shown striking the open fourth string. It's important to keep your hand steady and let your thumb make all the movement.

Top tip!
Don't forget to hold down the full shape when you're picking out notes from (or adding them to) a chord. For example, when playing the low G bass note against the C chord (bars 5 and 6), move your third finger onto the sixth string without disturbing the chord shape.

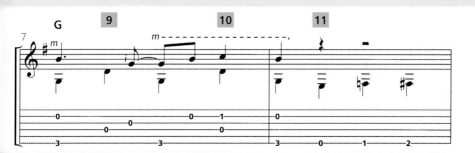

As you add the high C note with your first finger, your third finger should remain in position on the low G.

An ascending bassline rises chromatically from the open low E in this bar. Pick all of the notes with your thumb.

There's often no need to fret the full chord shape when you're fingerpicking. In this instance, the third finger (low G) and fourth finger (high D) fret only the notes required for the opening pinch.

As you pick the D bass note with your thumb, your first finger (i) should already be in position, ready to pick the third string.

Here, the thumb and second finger (m) are shown correctly playing the pinch on the fourth beat of the bar.

Only the third finger is actually fretting a note (the low G). Your remaining fingers should be positioned just above the strings, ready to play the next fretted notes.

Pick the pinch on the fourth beat with your thumb and first finger.

The full D7/F# chord should be fretted at the start of the bar. Your second finger frets the low F# while your first and second fingers fret the second and third strings respectively.

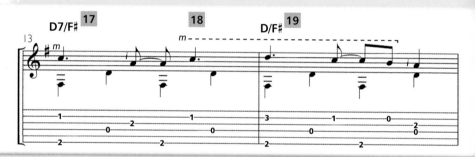

As you pick the C on the second string, your thumb should already be in position above the fourth string for the D bass note that follows.

Add the high D melody note on the second string with your fourth finger. The remaining fingers (including your first) should remain in position.

The G chord at the beginning of this bar is played by picking the strings simultaneously with your thumb, first finger (i) and second finger (m).

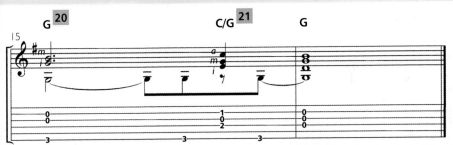

The upper notes of the C/G chord are played at the same time, using only your fingers (i, m and a).

Lesson 17
Alternating thumb bass

The logical next step after root and fifth bass notes, this technique is perfect for harmonizing bluesy melodies.

Alternating bass picking patterns have been a feature of acoustic blues guitar ever since Robert Johnson made his pact with the devil in Rosedale, Mississippi. Johnson allegedly pledged his soul in exchange for his exceptional talent. Whether you subscribe to this Southern voodoo or not, there's no denying that he remains one of the most influential of the Delta blues guitarists, long after his premature death (also shrouded in folklore and mystery) in 1938. So no need to go wandering around a crossroads at midnight in search of Beelzebub himself; grab your guitar, read on and leave your soul intact!

Finding the minor seventh of a chord

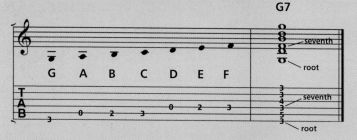

Alternating bass notes usually skip a string to play the octave of the root note or, as is common in blues accompaniments, the minor seventh. The minor seventh interval occurs in dominant seventh chords (i.e., E7, A7, etc.). You can double-check the note by counting up seven letter names (including the root). The minor seventh is always located a tone (two frets) below the octave, so you may have to lower your seventh by a half step to minorize it. The diagram above illustrates how to identify the minor seventh in a G7 chord.

The chords you'll need for this lesson:

E7

E7

A7   5fr.

Exercise 1
(Listen to track 27)

To get you started, this is a simple root/minor seventh bassline with a pinched melody note on the first beat of each bar. A different picking hand finger is used for each bar.

Play the opening pinch of this exercise with your thumb and third finger (a).

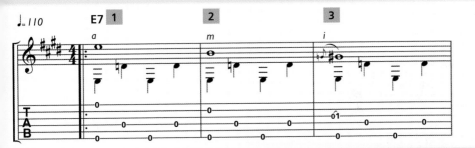

The pinch at the beginning of the second bar is played with your thumb and second finger (m).

Play the hammer-on to the G# with your first finger (i). Notice how the second finger is fretting the B on the fifth string. This way, if the string is accidentally played it will not result in a discordant note being sounded...

4

...and the same approach is used in bar 4.
Although only open strings are picked from the
chord, the full shape should still be fretted.

Top tip!
Remember that you should always palm
mute the bass notes by resting the fleshy
part of your picking hand palm gently
on the bass strings at the bridge. This
prevents the bass notes from ringing into
each other, which would sound messy.

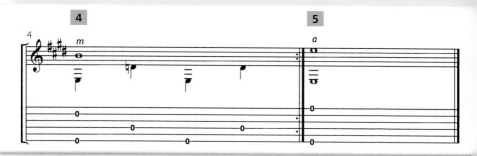

4   **5**

5

Play the final pinch
with your thumb
and third finger (a).

Exercise 2
(Listen to track 28)
This syncopated pattern is slightly more tricky than the previous example. Again, all three picking hand fingers (i, m and a) are given a workout.

Before you pick the first note, make sure you're fretting the full E7 chord shape. The first finger has been lifted off the string to allow the hammer-on to be played.

Pick the open first string (high E) using your third finger (a).

Use your first finger (i) to re-pick the open third string at the end of the first bar.

Exercise 3
(Listen to track 29)

When a picking pattern is applied to a barre chord, fretting hand pressure can be released between notes for more percussive and rhythmic results. In this example, try releasing your hand pressure briefly after the first and third beats to create the rests indicated.

The full A7 barre chord should be in position before you play the opening pinch. Although the fourth finger looks as if it's fretting the second string, it's actually hovering above it.

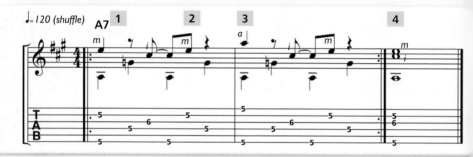

As you pick the second string with your second finger (m), bring your thumb into position, ready to play the fourth string.

At the start of the second bar, play the opening pinch with your thumb and third finger (a).

Pictured here with his famous resonator acoustic, Eddie James – also known as Son House – was a pioneer of the fingerpicked Delta blues style.

4

The concluding A7 chord should be played with a simultaneous pinch using your thumb, first finger (i) and second finger (m).

Top tip!
A shuffle is technically a 12/8 groove but, since this is a more complex time signature to write in, most shuffle blues are written in 4/4. The term "shuffle" is written at the start of the piece to indicate that quavers should be swung and not played straight. Listen to the CD to see how this should sound.

Lesson 18
Homesick Blues

In this lesson you'll learn a complete blues tune, incorporating the alternating thumb bass technique.

In the previous lesson you learned how to identify, locate and play the perfect minor seventh interval; you also learned how to use this interval to create a bassline that can be used with dominant seventh chords. Here you'll use this technique to play an original fingerpicking arrangement inspired by the great Delta blues guitarists of the early 20th century.

This will be the most challenging piece so far, so don't forget those all-important guidelines for learning a new arrangement:

- Break the tune down into manageable sections.
- Divide each section into two parts: melody (stems up) and bass notes (stems down).
- And last, but not least, give yourself time to learn – don't expect to be able to play new material instantly.

Before you add the bass notes to the melody, don't forget to check which melody notes are pinched and which are syncopated.

First and second time endings

First and second time endings are very common. On the first play-through of the piece you play the first time ending (bracketed and labelled "1"). This is usually followed by a repeat bar that sends you back to the beginning of the section. On the second play-through you skip the first time bar and jump straight to the second time ending.

The chords you'll need for this lesson:

E7	A/E	E7 (no 3rd)	A7	B7	B7

Example
(Listen to track 30)

This piece opens with a pinch on the third and sixth strings. This should be played with your thumb and first finger (i).

> **Top tip!**
> There are three chord symbols in parentheses in the first bar of this piece. These should be cross-referenced with the shapes given on page 94. Normally an E7 chord symbol would be all you would see in this bar.

Immediately after pinching the third and fifth string double stop, play the open first string (E) by picking it with your third finger (a).

Use your second finger for the slide from B to A on the third string. This ensures that you end up with your correct finger on the second fret.

Move your hand up the neck so that you can play the double stop on the second beat of this bar with your first and third fingers.

Flick your second finger sideways as you release it from the string to create a clear pull-off to the open G.

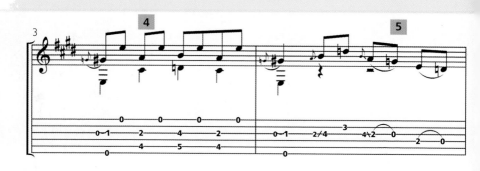

Classic blues albums:

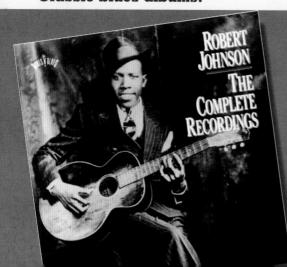

ROBERT JOHNSON
The Complete Recordings (1990)

The single most important guitarist in the evolution of blues guitar, Johnson only cut a handful of tracks and they're all on this collection.

MUDDY WATERS
The Anthology (2000)

A "must have" box set of the "King of Chicago Blues'" greatest tunes. Muddy

Use your thumb and first finger (i) to simultaneously pinch the third and fourth strings on the second beat.

Place your fourth finger on the eighth fret of the second string to add the high G to the basic A7 shape.

was a true blues pioneer, and one of the earliest musicians to make the switch to electric guitar.

HOWLIN' WOLF
The Definitive Collection (2007)

Another key Blues musician, many of Howlin' Wolf's most famous tunes were riff-based; this made him an influential figure among the pioneering rock guitarists of the 1960s.

JOHN LEE HOOKER
The Best of John Lee Hooker (1992)

Nineteen scorching blues classics from the man who popularized the Delta blues sound. John Lee Hooker's driving guitar riffs and distinctive vocals have influenced generations of musicians.

CONTINUED OVER THE PAGE ☞

The palm of your picking hand should be gently resting on the bass strings just in front of the bridge. This helps to "tame" the bass notes and prevent them from overpowering the melody.

Keep your second finger on the third string as you play the high D with your first finger. It will then be in position, ready for the slide to the A on the third beat.

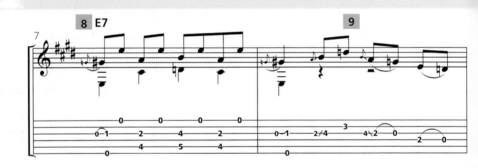

Classic blues albums (continued):

T-BONE WALKER
Stormy Monday Blues:
The Essential Collection (1998)

West Coast blues artist T-Bone Walker was a true pioneer of the electric guitar. His licks, riffs and playing style influenced many famous players, including Chuck Berry and Jimi Hendrix.

ERIC BIBB
The Good Stuff (1998)

Relative newcomer Eric Bibb is one of the most important blues artists to emerge in the last 20 years. In the UK, *The Times* newspaper described him as having "a voice to die for". This 1998 release is among his best.

Although only the low note is sounded on the first beat, the full B7 barre chord shape should be in position on the seventh fret before you play it...

...then slide the shape back down to the fifth fret for the A7 chord that follows.

BB KING

The Ultimate Collection (2005)

BB King is probably the most recognized of all the great bluesmen; his emotive guitar playing and incredible voice earned worldwide fame. Listen to this recommended album and you'll see why!

b.b. king the ultimate collection

On the second beat of bar 11 a chromatic slide
is played with the first and second fingers. Start
with your first finger on the third fret.

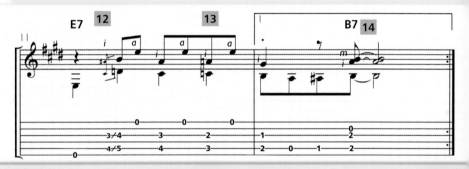

As you pick the last double stop in this bar
(using your thumb and first finger), your third
finger (a) should already be in position, ready
to pick the open E that follows.

Play the B7 chord with a three-finger pinch
using your thumb, first finger (i) and second
finger (m).

Top tip!

If you see a dot above or below a note this indicates that the note should be played "staccato". Staccato notes should be cut short instead of being allowed to ring for their full value. The opposite of staccato is "legato", which is indicated by a line above or below a note. Legato notes should be allowed to ring for their maximum written value.

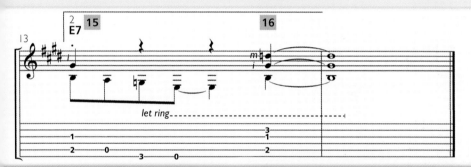

The dot above the E7 chord indicates that it should be played staccato. Release the pressure of your fretting fingers (without taking them off the strings) to mute the notes.

Be careful not to touch the sixth string with your second finger (m) as you fret the final E7 chord. The low E should be allowed to ring into the chord, as the "let ring" indicates.

SEE ALSO Harmonizing minor melodies, page 116

Lesson 19
Harmonizing major melodies

Learn how to harmonize a major melody in any key – the secrets of the pros revealed!

Without an understanding of chord progressions, how they work and where chords themselves come from, the whole business of accompanying can seem to be shrouded in mystery. To the uninitiated, professional musicians seem to be able to pluck chords from the ether with no rationale to explain how they did it. In fact, the concept of harmonizing a melody is quite mundane and mathematical. It requires no special gift. When all else fails, you can always apply the tried and tested rule: "If it sounds right, it is right!"

Diatonic major chords

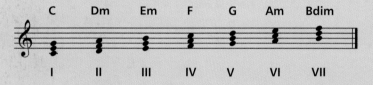

Diatonic essentially means "in the key of". In other words, a diatonic melody in C major would contain only notes from the C major scale. So diatonic chords are chords constructed only from the notes of the parent major scale, in this case C major. If you build a chord on each step of the major scale a distinct pattern of major, minor, and diminished chords is established. These diatonic chords are often described by musicians as numbers and written as Roman numerals. So, a simple progression such as C–F–C–G would be described as I–IV–I–V. Describing chords in this way not only makes the harmonic sequence instantly identifiable to another musician, it also makes it easy to transpose the progression to other keys.

The chords you'll need for this lesson:

Sale #32104

Created	Jun 18, 2021 13:43
Created By	Kris
Branch Address	4 Gwent Square, NP44 1PN
Branch Email	cwmbran@regenerate.co.uk
Branch Phone	01633 873332
Branch VAT #	908808793

Item	Price	Qty	Total
Behringer UM300 Ultra Metal * BBCW88F91CB20	£9.99	1	£9.99
	£9.99	1	£9.99

Payment	Amount
Cash	£9.99

* Second-hand goods are sold on a VAT margin scheme. No input tax is reclaimable on these items.

Second-hand goods sold on this invoice are sold on a VAT margin scheme. No input tax is therefore reclaimable. Buy With Confidence. Please note there is no refund on dvds, games or cds, 48 hour exchange only. Like us Facebook! Scan this code to take you to r Facebook Page

Joni Mitchell knows a thing or two about harmonizing major melodies; her stunning accompaniments have been influencing fingerpickers since the 1960s.

Exercise 1
(Listen to track 31)

This simple C major melody will be the subject of two harmonizations. Play the melody through a few times to get it "in your ear". It will help to sing or hum it, especially when you're adding some harmony.

When you're playing a melody on its own (i.e., with no bass notes), it's acceptable to rest your thumb on the sixth string as shown.

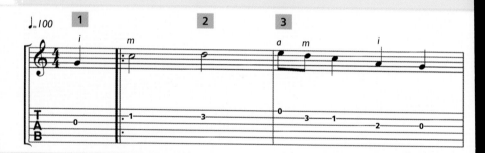

Here, the second finger (m) picks the second string. Although this follows the traditional "i, m, a on the top three strings" convention, you do not have to adhere to this religiously when playing an unaccompanied melody.

By picking the open first string with your third finger (a), you can quickly play the following note (D) with your second finger (m).

Pick the high C at the start of the third bar with your second finger (m). Notice that the thumb is firmly anchored on the sixth string.

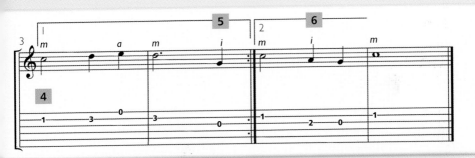

Use your first finger (i) to pick the open third string. This is the pick-up note for the second statement of the tune.

Just before the melody concludes, the closing notes are played on the third string. Use your first finger (i) to pick both the A and the open G that follows it.

Exercise 2
(Listen to track 32)
Your first harmonization uses what is
known as the "three chord trick". This
is nothing more than chords I–IV–V in a
major key. Literally thousands of songs
can be played with these three chords.

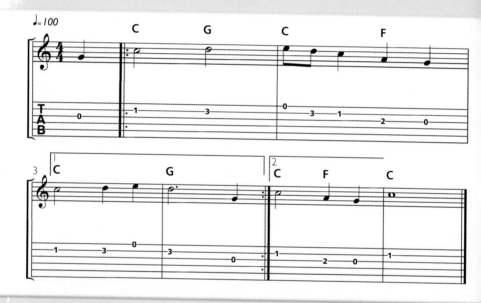

Top tip!
It's much easier to forget about fingerpicking patterns
when you're harmonizing a tune. Just play simple block
chords, i.e., strum the chords once with your thumb,
or pluck them using p, i, m, a simultaneously. Once
you've settled on a chord progression it will be much
easier to add the picking pattern.

Exercise 3
(Listen to track 33)

By adding diatonic minor chords to the sequence the melody gains a depth and sophistication that major chords alone cannot provide. Notice how the first melody note is always a chord tone, i.e., a note that can be found in the chord used to harmonize it.

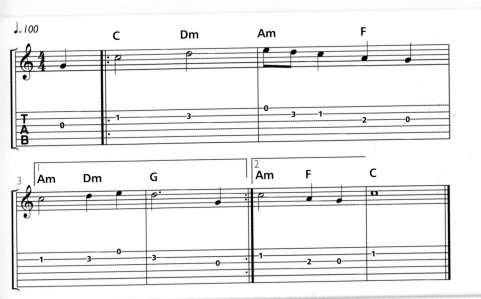

Top tip!

Even when you've got the sheet music, or you know the chord progression for a song, it's always worth experimenting with different chords. Try substituting a diatonic minor chord for a major. It's simple changes like this that musicians use to create their own distinctive arrangements of well-known songs.

Lesson 20
Morning Has Broken

Learn a complete fingerstyle guitar arrangement of this beautiful major melody in this lesson.

Even if you already know this tune, it's well worth taking time out to listen to the full arrangement on the CD first. It's also a good idea to listen to as many versions of a song as you can before you start working on it. (There are plenty of Internet sites that allow you to listen to music on demand and for free.) The arrangement makes good use of arpeggiated chords, so it's very important to be able to identify and emphasize the melody notes.

"Morning Has Broken" is believed to have been based on a traditional Irish tune. Celtic songs are perfect for fingerstyle guitar repertoire; the melodies are simple and rhythmical and ideal for creating original arrangements. If you want to explore this genre further, a good source of material is *O'Neill's Music of Ireland* (revised by Miles Krassen), which contains over 1,000 traditional fiddle melodies.

Top tips!

- Right-hand picking indication (i, m, a) is generally only given at the start of the bar. Unless indicated otherwise, always assume that you will play repeated notes with the same fingers. This avoids cluttering the arrangement with too much information.

- Although the chord shapes are given for this piece at the start of the lesson, it's not always necessary to fret the whole chord all of the time. Fretting only necessary notes will enable you to change chords more quickly and fluently.

The chords you'll need for this lesson:

G   Am   D   C   G/B   Bm

Famous recordings of this tune

"Morning Has Broken" is a traditional Christian hymn that was popularized by Cat Stevens in 1971. Often mistakenly credited to Stevens, the original composer remains unknown. The tune was first published in 1931 as an arrangement by composer Martin Shaw with lyrics by Eleanor Farjeon. Here are just a few of the eclectic mix of artists who have recorded this timeless melody:

CAT STEVENS
Teaser and the Firecat (1971)

KENNY ROGERS
Rollin' (1973)

NEIL DIAMOND
The Christmas Album (1992)

ART GARFUNKEL
Songs from a Parent to a Child (1997)

NANA MOUSKOURI
At Her Very Best (2001)

JUDY COLLINS
The Essential Judy Collins (2004)

AARON NEVILLE
Gospel Roots (2005)

ACKER BILK
The Magic Clarinet of Acker Bilk (2005)

Em	D/F#	D7/F#	A7	Am7	G
			2fr.		

Exercise
(Listen to track 34)

Play the second note of the pick-up bar by sliding your second finger (m) along the third string. The pitch is created by the sliding action alone – don't re-pick the string.

Fret the open G chord using only your third (a) and fourth fingers.

The Am chord should be fretted with a third finger barre across the top three strings on the fifth fret.

To play the open E on the second beat, lift off your second finger while keeping the remaining fingers of the D chord in position.

Play the pinch at the beginning of this bar with your thumb and third finger (a).

In this bar, your fingers move onto the lower strings so that the first finger (i) picks the fourth string, the second finger (m) picks the third string and the third finger (a) picks the second string.

This G chord should be fretted using only your third finger. Add the melody note A with your second finger as demonstrated.

The outer notes of the Bm chord should be pinched using the thumb and third finger (a); (i, m and a remain on the lower strings until the following bar).

For the Em chord, the fingers return to their more familiar "top three strings" positioning. The opening pinch in this bar can then be played with the thumb and third finger (a) as shown.

Pick the open second string with your third finger (a). Your second (m) and third (a) fingers are then used on the lower strings, as in the previous bars.

11

Pinch the first chord of this bar using your thumb (p), first (i) and second (m) fingers. Your fingers should form a "claw" shape.

12

Move your first (i) and second (m) fingers across the strings to pinch the last double stop in this bar.

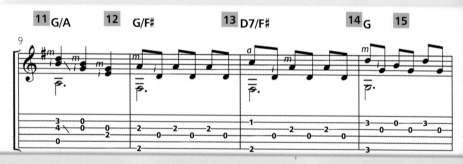

11 G/A   **12** G/F#   **13** D7/F#   **14** G   **15**

13

By fretting the full D7/F# chord shape at the start of bar 11, you will be free to concentrate on the picking pattern alone. This also allows the notes to ring clearly throughout both bars.

14

The G chord is fretted using only your third and fourth fingers on the sixth and second strings respectively...

15

...lift the fourth finger off the second string to allow the open B to sound on the second beat. The finger should be returned to the string on the third beat for the D note.

By adding your fourth finger (on the third fret of the first string) to a regular C chord, the high G melody note can easily be included in the chord shape...

...and by lifting the finger off the string in the following bar (but keeping the chord shape intact), the more familiar open E becomes the top voice of the C chord.

Play the opening pinch in this bar with your thumb and second finger (m).

In bar 16, the first (i) and second (m) fingers move onto the lower strings. Here you can clearly see the thumb, first and second fingers playing the opening pinch.

This unusual A7 shape is played across three strings. Use your fourth finger to fret the G on the fourth string and your first to fret the A on the third. The fifth string is played open.

The open second string should be sounded in this bar, so fret the D/F♯ chord using only your second and third fingers.

As you pick the last two open strings in the bar, your third and fourth fingers should be moving above their respective frets, ready for a smooth change to the G chord that quickly follows.

Play the pinched G chord using your thumb on the sixth string and your third finger (a) on the second string.

The pinch for the C chord in this bar returns the third finger (a) to the first string with the thumb picking the fifth string.

Play the pinched D/F♯ chord using your thumb to pick the sixth string and your second finger (m) to pick the third.

Fret the G/B chord using your second finger on the fifth string and your fourth on the third fret of the second string.

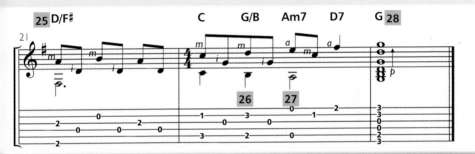

You don't need to fret a full Am7 shape here; just fret the C on the second string with your first finger as shown. Keep your third finger ready for the F♯ that quickly follows.

The final G chord is played by brushing your thumb across the strings from low to high (i.e., starting on the sixth string as shown).

SEE ALSO Harmonizing major melodies, page 102

Lesson 21
Harmonizing minor melodies

Now that you have a good understanding of harmonizing melodies in a major key, it's time to get to grips with those sad, minor keys.

It will take time and experience to become fluent at the art of harmonizing "on the fly", but you now have all the tools you need to get started. As you discovered in lesson 19, there is only one major scale; it generates a specific series of perfect and major intervals. Musicians use this pattern of intervals as a reference point when describing or analysing harmony. Harmonizing minor melodies is a little more complex. This is because there isn't one conclusive minor scale that can be used to generate diatonic minor chords. There are three basic minor scales: the natural minor (also known as the Aeolian mode); the harmonic

minor; and the melodic minor. Most minor key tunes are harmonized using a mixture of chords from all three scales.

This book aims to get you playing fingerstyle guitar quickly and efficiently, so there's no point in getting bogged down in theory. (There are plenty of websites out there dedicated to harmony and music theory.) To keep things simple, this lesson only looks at the diatonic chords for the natural minor scale (Aeolian mode). Notice how the Roman numerals beneath the chords are flattened on the third, sixth and seventh steps to reflect the minor intervals generated by the minor scale formulae.

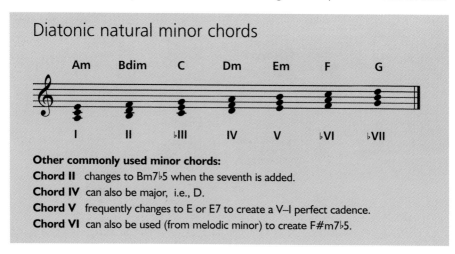

Diatonic natural minor chords

Am	Bdim	C	Dm	Em	F	G
I	II	♭III	IV	V	♭VI	♭VII

Other commonly used minor chords:
Chord II   changes to Bm7♭5 when the seventh is added.
Chord IV   can also be major, i.e., D.
Chord V   frequently changes to E or E7 to create a V–I perfect cadence.
Chord VI   can also be used (from melodic minor) to create F#m7♭5.

The chords you'll need for this lesson:

Dm

G

C

F

Bm7(♭5)

Exercise 1
(Listen to track 35)

This melody has a traditional feel that hints at many famous tunes. When you tap the beat as quavers, those tricky semiquavers will be easier to phrase accurately.

When playing quick phrases such as the pick-up measure in this piece, it's more efficient to alternate between your first (i) and second (m) fingers. Here, you can see the first finger (i) playing the first note of the pick-up…

…quickly followed by the second finger (m) picking the second note on the first string.

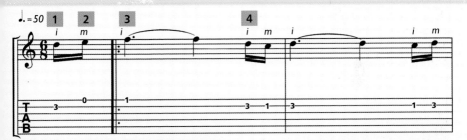

The first string is then re-picked at the start of the first bar using the first finger (i).

To ensure that the first finger (i) always plays the "on-beat" notes, it should also be used to pick the second string on beat six.

In bar 3 the open first string is picked with the first finger (i).

Again, on beat six, the second string is picked with the same finger to preserve the pattern of "first finger on the beat, second finger off the beat" picking.

On the last off beat of bar 4, make sure you are using your second finger (m) to pick the second string.

There are exceptions to every rule! So when you pick the first note on beat six of bar 5, start as before on your first finger (i)...

...but then, because it's quicker to "drag" the finger across the strings when picking across two adjacent strings, use the same finger (i) to play the third string.

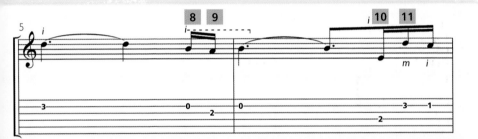

The off beat rule is ignored again when playing the fourth string in bar 6. Here, you can see the first finger (i) being used to pick the string...

...but the following note involves a string jump back to the second string, so play it with your second finger (m) as shown, even though it falls on the sixth beat.

The first note of the first time ending should be picked with your first finger (i).

The last two notes in bar 8 are the same as those in the pick-up bar at the start of the tune, so the same fingering is used. Here, the first finger (i) is shown picking the first note (on the second string).

James Taylor frequently played with a capo, as you can see here. To change the key of your minor accompaniments, check out the Capo Keys (pages 230–249).

Exercise 2
(Listen to track 36)
The harmonization of this tune is based on a popular cycle of fifths progression (i.e., with each subsequent chord occurring a fifth higher). Notice the A major chord at the end of the first time bar. This is functioning as the dominant (V) of the Dm. It pushes the progression back to the start of the sequence.

Fret the Dm chord using your fourth finger on the second string. This will enable you to change quickly and smoothly to the following chord.

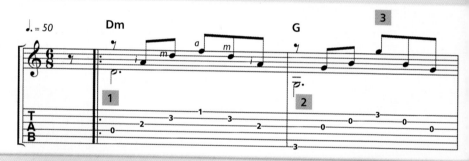

At the start of bar 2, the G chord can be fretted using only your third finger on the sixth string...

...then simply add your fourth finger on the first string to add the high G note. (Keep your third finger in position to allow the bass note to ring.)

Strike the root note of the C chord using your thumb. Notice that the remaining fingers (i, m and a) are already in position above their respective strings.

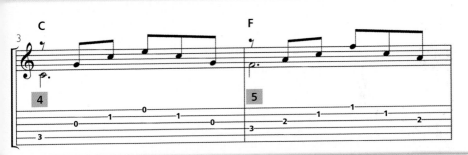

The bass note of the F chord is played on the fourth string with your thumb.

The Bm7(♭5) chord in bar 5 sounds intimidating but it's really just a Dmin shape with the low B added on the fifth string. Use your second finger to fret the low note.

The E7 chord in bar 6 is a "condensed" four-note voicing. Fret the chord using your first, second and fourth fingers. (The third finger hovers above the strings.)

The Am/C chord in bar 8 bears no relation to the more familiar Am shape. Fret the fifth string with your second finger and the third string with your first finger.

Top tips!

The fingerpicking arrangement here doesn't include the tune. Once you can play it confidently, play along with exercise I on the CD (track 35).

The last chord in this sequence is E7. It is not diatonic to the natural minor scale, but is taken instead from the harmonic minor. It provides a more satisfactory conclusion to the sequence than a simple Em chord would. Try strumming along to track 35 (melody only) and substitute Em for E7 – you'll instantly hear the difference.

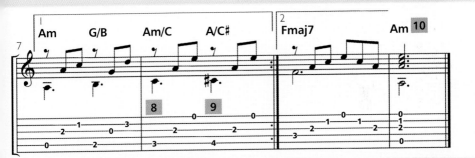

When you change to the A/C♯ chord on the fourth beat, simply add your third finger to the fifth string. (Keep the first finger on the third string throughout.)

The final Am chord is played with the thumb and all three picking fingers (i, m and a) simultaneously.

Lesson 22
Scarborough Fair

An original arrangement of this timeless tune demonstrates how to create an effective accompaniment for a minor melody.

Think of Scarborough and you'll probably also think "English seaside resort", but during the Middle Ages it was the business capital of Europe. Traders travelled from far and wide to attend the annual 45-day trade fair, which was traditionally held in August; hence the title of this famous tune, which has a long history dating back to the 17th century. It is incredible that a simple, anonymous melody like this has survived for so long. Originally folk tunes would have been passed from musician to musician – there were no recordings, sheet music or digital downloads! "Scarborough Fair" is a simple, lilting tune that transcends genres and fashions; ask anyone to name a famous folk tune and chances are they'll cite this one.

This classic tune – which featured in the controversial film
The Graduate **– was made famous by Simon and Garfunkel.**

The chords you'll need for this lesson:

Am

E

C

Am 5fr.

G/B

Famous recordings of this tune

The most famous version has to be Simon and Garfunkel's recording, released in 1966. Paul Simon apparently learned the tune from folk singer/guitarist Martin Carthy on a trip to London in 1965. The duo's reworking was a big departure from the original and didn't credit the traditional origins of the tune either! Opposite are some of the diverse artists that have covered this tune.

SIMON AND GARFUNKEL
Parsley, Sage, Rosemary & Thyme (1966)

MARIANNE FAITHFULL
Northern Maid (1966)

WES MONTGOMERY
Road Song (1968)

JUSTIN HAYWARD
Classic Blue (1989)

SERGIO MENDES AND BRASIL '66
Greatest Hits (1990)

MARTIN CARTHY
Classic Carthy (2001)

HERBIE HANCOCK
The New Standard (2005)

Exercise
(Listen to track 37)

Hold down the full Am chord shape throughout the first two bars to allow the notes to ring into each other.

The pinch at the beginning of bar 2 should be played with your thumb and third finger (a).

To play the C note that is added to the chord on the second beat, simply flatten your first finger onto the second string.

As you pick the fourth string with your thumb, ensure that your remaining fingers (i, m and a) remain above their respective strings.

To add the high G to the C chord on beat 3, simply fret the note with your fourth finger (without taking your remaining fingers off the strings).

The Am chord in bar 6 should be played with a barre across the fifth fret using your third finger (a).

The double-stop phrase that begins at the end of bar 6 should be picked with your thumb and second finger (i), while the first finger hovers above the strings.

The double-stop phrase moves onto the lower strings at the end of bar 7; use the same picking as before (i.e., your thumb and second finger).

As you strike the sixth string with your thumb, the full E chord shape should be in position.

The Am chord in bar 10 should be played with a barre across the fifth fret using your third finger (a)...

...followed by a quick jump to the second fret (using your first finger) to play the melody note on the third beat.

For a smooth change from C to G/B use your second and fourth fingers to fret the G/B chord.

The C chord on the first beat of bar 12 should be played with your first finger (fifth string) and fourth finger (second string). Take care not to touch the third string, since this will prevent it from sounding.

Throughout bars 13 and 14 the G chord can be fretted with just the third finger on the sixth string…

…and then the A note at the end of bar 14 can be added with your second finger (while keeping your third finger on the low G).

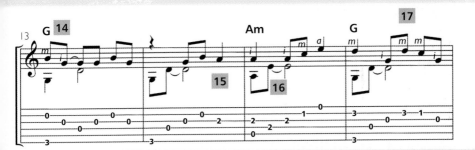

Play the pinch at the beginning of bar 15 with your thumb and first finger (i).

The G chord in this bar is played with your third finger (sixth string) and fourth finger (second string). Here, you can see the first finger in position on the first fret, ready to play the C note on the third beat.

To add the A note to the E chord, simply place
your fourth finger in front of your first finger
on the second fret (without taking the first
finger off the string).

Top tip!
Don't stick too rigidly to the
chord shapes when you're
working on this arrangement;
the tune is very classical in
style, and so is based on a
counterpoint approach rather
than blocks of harmony. You
may find the piece easier to
learn if you think of it as two
simultaneous melody lines.

As you play the open string pinch on the first
beat of this bar, your fingers should be moving
up the neck to fret the chord shape...

...which should be played with your first and
second fingers. Take care not to damp the open
third string by inadvertently touching it with
your second finger.

Play the pinch at the beginning of bar 20 with your thumb and second finger (m).

Top tip!
The melody of this tune needs to be accented slightly to make it stand out from the arpeggio notes that surround it. Keep listening to the recording as you work through the arrangement; you will notice more detail as you progress through the piece.

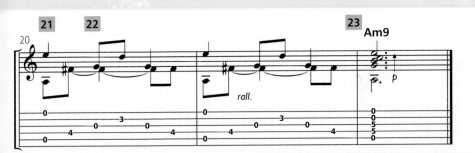

Pick out the open third string using your first finger (i). Notice that the second finger (m) is in position above the second string, ready for the high D that follows.

The final Am chord is played by brushing your thumb across the strings (low to high).

SEE ALSO
Alternating thumb bass, page 88

Lesson 23
Playing riffs

Riffs have been a feature of popular music since the early days of jazz and blues. In this lesson you'll learn how to create them.

Without riffs, every genre of popular music would sound bland and lifeless. Whether we're talking subtle bass riffs or full band unison riffs, they are the mainstay of popular music. Can you imagine any style of rock music without riffs? The guitar (acoustic or electric) is perfect for playing riffs; that's why some of the most memorable ones have been guitar based. From the early Delta blues riffs of Robert Johnson to the pioneering work of the post British blues boom bands such as Cream and Led Zeppelin,

you could be forgiven for thinking that all the best riffs had already been written! However, the endless combinations of rhythm and pitch, plus the individual playing style of each guitarist, thankfully mean that this is not the case. Blues, in particular, is enjoying a resurgence of popularity at the moment with a wealth of talent breathing new life into the genre. Great music transcends fads and fashions, proving that this timeless music (now well over 100 years old) ain't ready for the old folks' home just yet!

Where do riffs come from?

The minor blues scale

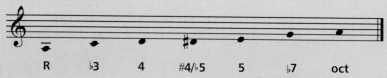

| R | ♭3 | 4 | #4/♭5 | 5 | ♭7 | oct |

The best riffs are short and simple; these are also the hardest ones to conceive. The Rolling Stones set the music world on fire with the release of their single "Satisfaction" back in 1965. Yet this iconic riff comprises just three notes! It's the choice of notes that, when coupled with a syncopated rhythm, creates the wow factor that hooks in the listener. Many guitarists use the minor pentatonic and minor blues scale as a note source for riffs; Cream's "Sunshine of Your Love", Jimi Hendrix's "Purple Haze", and Deep Purple's unforgettable "Smoke on the Water" are just three examples.

The chords you'll need for this lesson:

A5	A7	G5	Gm7	C5/G
	5fr.		3fr.	3fr.

Known for his energetic performances and complex fingerpicking style, Tommy Emmanuel was an expert at picking out great riffs.

Exercise 1

(Listen to track 38)
Fingerstyle players have a distinct advantage over pick players when it comes to playing riffs. In this example a crotchet bass riff is played against a syncopated power chord (A5).

The opening hammer-on is picked with your thumb, which should strike the fourth string firmly and cleanly.

Use your first (i) and second fingers (m) to pick the double stop on the first off beat of bar 1.

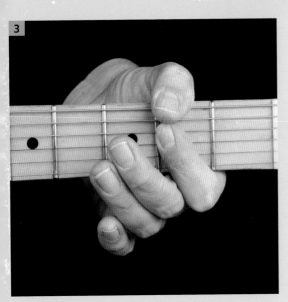

Bring your thumb around the back of the neck and onto the sixth string to play the bass note on the third beat.

Top tips!
• When you're trying to come up with new ideas for riffs, always have a quick and simple recording device to hand. (There are loads of small and affordable devices on the market.) It's best to capture an idea quickly before it's forgotten. Stopping to write ideas down or waiting for your computer to boot up just takes too long, man!

• The first two riffs in this lesson should be played with "swing" quavers. This is exactly the same feel as the 12/8 shuffle groove explained in lesson 17. Always listen to the full track on the CD before you start, to make sure you understand the groove you're aiming for.

At the end of the first bar the middle strings are re-picked using the first (i) and second (m) fingers. Notice that the thumb is in position, ready to play the next bass note on the fifth string.

Exercise 2
(Listen to track 39) Adding an alternating bass pattern to a simple, syncopated melody part is a great way to create cool riffs like this one.

Pick the first melody note on the third string using your first finger (i).

Fret the double stop on the second beat using your first finger (third string) and third finger (fourth string).

The first double stop in bar 2 should be fretted with your first finger (fourth string) and third finger (second string)...

...and then slide the shape one fret higher and add your second finger on the second string.

Exercise 3
(Listen to track 40)

In this piece, a static quaver bassline underpins two-note chords (double stops) to create a classic rock-style riff.

Play the low G on the sixth string with your first finger.

By flattening your first finger across all six strings you can barre the middle strings for the Gm7 chord on the second beat.

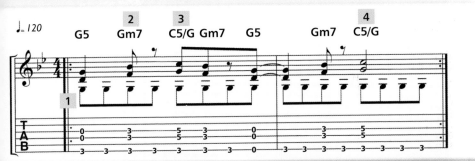

Release the barre (but keep fretting the sixth string) and place your third finger across the middle strings on the fifth fret for the C5/G.

Keep your first and third fingers in position until the end of the second bar. This will allow the C5 chord to ring as you pick out the G bass notes.

Lesson 24
The Gallows Pole

Learn how to incorporate riffs into your tunes with an original arrangement of this haunting folk ballad.

Based on a traditional folk song, "The Maid Freed from the Gallows", this ballad was first recorded as "The Gallows Pole" by the blues singer Leadbelly in 1939. Many artists have released their own versions of the tune, and it was famously featured on the album "Led Zeppelin III" in 1970. The original folk song was written from the perspective of a condemned woman pleading with her executioners, begging them to wait for the various friends and relatives she imagines will save her. Leadbelly's version added a male perspective to the lyric. The Led Zeppelin version added a further twist: the hangman accepts all the bribes, but still performs the execution. That's rock 'n' roll for you!

The riff in this arrangement kicks off the tune, features as a short interlude before the repeat and also provides a dramatic ending. It's important to remember that a riff should be repeated throughout your arrangement for maximum effect; it's this repetition that grabs the listeners' attention.

Led Zeppelin guitarist Jimmy Page adapted "The Gallow's Pole" from a version by Fred Gerlach, to create what was, perhaps, the most famous cover version.

The chords you'll need for this lesson:

Gm	Gm	Bb6	C5
			3fr.

Famous recordings of this tune

LEADBELLY
The Earliest Blues Guitarists (2008)

ODETTA
Maybe She Go (2008)

JOE BROWN
Down to Earth (2006)

LONG JOHN BALDRY
Remembering Leadbelly (2001)

ROY METTÉ
12 Bars and the Blues (2005)

TEX RITTER
Country Classics (2000)

JULIAN MOKHTAR
About Time (1999)

LED ZEPPELIN
Led Zeppelin III (1970)

This traditional folk song was reintroduced into mainstream 20th-century culture by the bluesman Leadbelly. It's worth checking out his version to hear the frenetic fingerpicking he uses to accompany himself (played on a 12-string guitar). The Led Zeppelin version contains multi-layered guitar parts (six- and 12-string acoustic, banjo and electric guitar) played by Zep's virtuouso guitarist Jimmy Page.

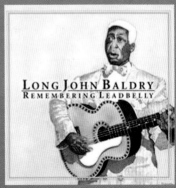

Exercise
(Listen to track 41)

The first G chord is played with an F bass note on the first fret. This should be fretted with your first finger,...

...which leaves your third finger free to fret the G bass note that quickly follows.

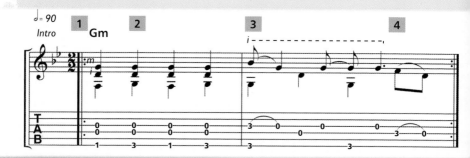

Add the B♭ on the third string with your fourth finger, releasing it with a sideways flicking motion to create the pull-off to the open G.

Add the F on the fourth string with your fourth finger, releasing it with a sideways flicking motion to create the pull-off to the open D. Keep your third finger in position throughout.

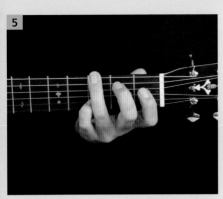

Fret the double stop on beat one of bar 3 using your third finger (sixth string) and fourth finger (second string).

Top tip!
The chord shapes (particularly Gm) at the start of the lesson should be interpreted as a guide only. This piece superimposes the tune against a continuous alternating bass pattern, so there aren't many actual chord shapes as such.

While keeping your third finger on the low G, add the C on the second string with your first finger...

...then quickly add your fourth finger on the third string to play the B♭ that follows.

Although the second string should be picked with the second finger (m), when playing quick successive notes it's better to use alternate fingers. Here, the first finger (i) plays the second D note on beat two.

Top tip!
You'll have noticed the unusual 2/2 time signature at the start of this piece. Up-tempo tunes such as this one are often written in 2/2 as opposed to 4/4 time. There are still four crotchets in every bar; they'll just feel like quavers when you're tapping your foot in a minim pulse!

Fret the pinch on the third beat using your third finger (sixth string) and first finger (second string). Your fourth finger should already be above the third string for the B♭ that follows.

Playing the C# to the D with a slide is a little tricky! Fret the first note with your second finger and slide it under the third finger to play the D.

Remember that consecutive notes on the same string are easier to play with alternate picking fingers. So pick the first open G in bar 7 with your first finger...

...and play the pinch with your thumb and middle finger (m).

Fret the opening double stop in bar 8 using your third finger (sixth string) and second finger (second string)...

...then lift off your second finger and add your first finger on the first fret for the C melody note that quickly follows. Notice the fourth finger in position above the third string, ready for the B♭.

The low pinch on beat one of this bar is played with your thumb (p – on the fifth string) and first finger (i – on the fourth string).

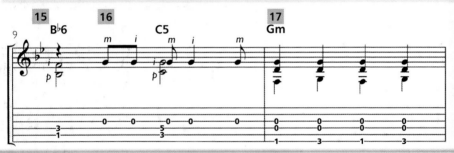

The open third string is picked with your second finger (m). The repeated note should then be played with your first finger (i).

The three-note chords should be picked using the thumb, first (i) and second (m) fingers simultaneously.

Play the B♭6 chord using your first and third fingers. Remember to keep your third finger slightly angled so that it doesn't mute the open third string.

Slide your fingers up two frets to play the C5 on beat three. Always avoid taking your fingers off the strings when you're moving a chord shape – just release the pressure of your fingers to facilitate the movement.

SEE ALSO Open chord shapes, page 34;
Moveable chord shapes, page 50

Lesson 25
Major sevenths and exotic dominant chords

Here are some essential major seventh and exotic dominant chord shapes that can be played in any key.

You haven't looked at chord shapes in a while, so in this lesson you'll be looking at some sophisticated chords that will add a touch of class and a dash of colour to your arrangements. The chords in this lesson won't present such a steep learning curve as the barre chords back in lesson 14 – at least as far as the playing side of things goes. Their names may look a little scary, but these are all sounds that you'll have heard before. There are no superfluous shapes here either, just useful voicings that can be applied to

a wide range of genres and musical scenarios.

We've looked at minor seventh and dominant seventh chords before, but not at the jazzy-sounding major seventh chord. All five shapes are given here. The strangely named dominant seventh chords are also cool, jazzy-sounding chords. All of these chords are great for creating sophisticated arrangements. You'll get a chance to use some of them in the next two lessons, where you'll be exploring Latin-style accompaniments.

Creating seventh chords

1) minor seventh   2) dominant seventh   3) major seventh

Chords are created by stacking major and/or minor thirds on top of each other (see lesson 8). The diagram here illustrates how the three different types of seventh chords are constructed: a minor third stacked above a minor triad creates a minor seventh chord; a minor third above a major triad creates a dominant seventh chord; and finally a major third above a major triad creates the sweet-sounding major seventh chord.

Mississippi John Hurt was an influential country blues singer and guitarist, who was no stranger to jazzy sounding chord arrangements.

Example 1

**Five moveable major
seventh chord shapes**

The five major seventh
shapes shown are derived
from the CAGED system,
which is based on the five
open major chord shapes. All
of these chords are in root
position (i.e., with the lowest
note giving the name of the
chord) except for the last
shape, which is in second
inversion (where the fifth is
the lowest note).

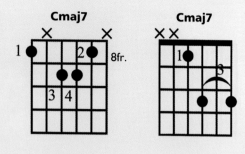

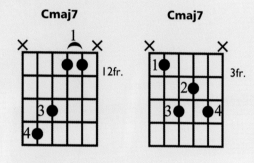

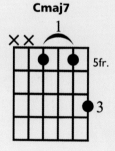

Top tip!

Just because a chord has an
exotic name, it doesn't mean
that it's the sole preserve
of jazz musicians! Don't be
afraid to experiment – try
incorporating these chords
into your own arrangements.
As mentioned previously: "If
it sounds right, it is right!"

Example 2
Six exotic dominant chords

More exciting-sounding dominant seventh chords can be achieved simply by altering the fifth of the chord (i.e., #5 and ♭5), or adding "extensions" to the chord, such as the ninth, eleventh or thirteenth. All of these chords have the root as their lowest note.

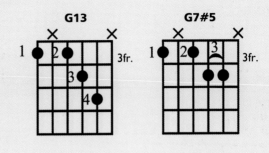

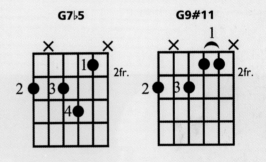

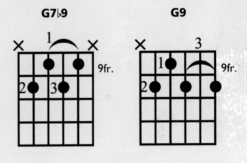

Top tip!

All of the fingerings shown are intended as a guide – they are not set in stone! There will be instances when you'll find that a different fingering could be more effective (e.g. when using your thumb to fret a bass note).

Lesson 26
Latin American rhythms

SEE ALSO
Alternating thumb bass, page 88

Cool, sophisticated bossa nova accompaniments sound fantastic on the guitar. Learn how to play them in this lesson.

The gently lilting bossa nova rhythms are ideal for electric or acoustic guitar. The music was pioneered in the mid-1950s by Brazilian musicians Antônio Carlos Jobim and João Gilberto, and then "discovered" by jazz guitarist Charlie Byrd while on tour in Latin America during the late 1950s. Byrd made bossa nova fashionable all over the world when he teamed up with saxophonist Stan Getz to record his famous album "Jazz Samba". The original bossa nova rhythms were played fingerstyle on a classical, nylon-strung guitar. Today, they are more likely to be played on electric guitar with a mellow, clean tone. Whichever guitar you decide to play these on, they're guaranteed to infuse your playing with cool Latin flavours.

Charlie Byrd, the original bossa nova maestro, pictured here picking out a cool Latin comp on a nylon string guitar.

The chords you'll need for this lesson:

Classic bossa nova recordings

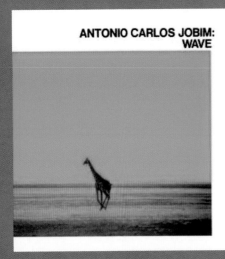

ANTONIO CARLOS JOBIM: WAVE

Learning any style of music should involve as much listening as practice. You'll probably find yourself wanting to hear more of this great music once you've played the examples in this lesson. So here is a list of the classic recordings that started the whole 1960s bossa nova movement, beginning with Charlie Byrd and Stan Getz's number one album of 1962.

CHARLIE BYRD/STAN GETZ
Jazz Samba (1962)

Featuring the compositions of Brazilian composer Antônio Carlos Jobim and the exquisite accompaniments of guitarist Charlie Byrd, this album quickly established the bossa nova as a worldwide movement on its release in 1962.

STAN GETZ/JOÃO GILBERTO
Getz/Gilberto (1964)

Brazilian vocalist/guitarist Gilberto collaborated with saxophonist Getz in 1964 to produce this outstanding album. It contains many songs that remain the mainstay of the Latin/jazz repertoire to this day, including "The Girl From Ipanema", "Corcovado" and "Desafinado".

ANTÔNIO CARLOS JOBIM
Wave (1967)

The inclusion of Jobim's tunes on many American jazz albums enabled him to establish his own solo career in the USA. Wave was Jobim's third solo album and was released in 1967. It showcases not only his beautiful compositions, but also his formidable arranging skills.

FRANK SINATRA AND ANTÔNIO CARLOS JOBIM
Francis Alberto Sinatra & Antônio Carlos Jobim (1967)

Frank Sinatra was quick to realise the importance of the 1960s bossa nova movement, and released this collaboration with Jobim in 1967. Nominated for a Grammy in 1968, it also includes standards from the Great American Songbook, arranged in the bossa-nova style.

Exercise 1
(Listen to track 42)
This is the standard bossa nova rhythm for creating Latin accompaniments. It is derived from the clava patterns of the faster and more complex samba. Release the grip of your fretting hand between chords to keep them short, as indicated.

The Dm7 chord should be played using all of your picking hand fingers. The thumb strikes the string from the side while the fingers pick simultaneously in a clawlike motion.

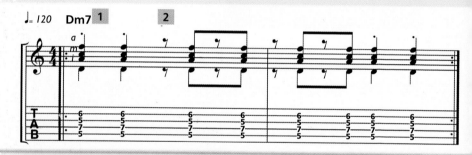

It's important to play rests as well as notes! The rests are created by releasing the pressure of your fretting hand, but without taking the fingers off the strings.

Top tips!
• The bossa nova rhythm is heavily syncopated and avoids the first beat of the second bar, making it a tricky comp to master – especially when you're adding a minim bassline into the mix. Start slowly and use a metronome to keep in time.

• When it's not practical to add the fifth in a bassline (i.e., when playing a ♯5 chord or adding an awkward melody note), just repeat the root note on the third beat. This wouldn't sound good on every chord, but is permissible when used sparingly.

Antônio Carlos Jobim was not only one of the most important songwriters of the 1960s, he was also a master of the Latin style guitar.

Exercise 2
(Listen to track 43)

By adding a root and fifth bassline on beats one and three the complete bossa nova rhythm is created. Playing this syncopated pattern against a minim bass pattern is not easy – so don't rush this one!

On the first beat of bar 1, the chord and bass note are sounded together. The strings are picked simultaneously using your thumb and fingers (i, m and a).

On the second beat, only the chord notes should be sounded. Here the fingers (i, m and a) can be seen picking the second, third and fourth strings simultaneously.

On the first beat of the second bar, only the bass note should be played. Use your thumb to strike the fifth string.

The penultimate chord is sounded with a low A in the bass. Use your thumb and fingers (i, m and a) simultaneously.

Exercise 3
(Listen to track 44)

Because the bossa nova rhythm is a two-bar pattern, care must be taken when a chord change falls on the second bar. Notice how the chord change is anticipated at the end of bar 1, but the bass note is not sounded until beat one of bar 2.

Just as in the previous examples, the opening chord and bass note should be sounded together, using the thumb and fingers (i, m and a) to pick all four notes simultaneously.

In order to anticipate the chord change on the off beat, the G13 chord should be fretted just ahead of the second bar. Notice the first finger is barring across all six strings so that the low G can be included in the chord.

Keep the chord shape intact, even when playing the bass note on the fifth string on beat three.

SEE ALSO **Latin American rhythms, page 152**

Lesson 27
Latin workout

Learn this original bossa nova arrangement and exercise your newly acquired comping skills.

Antônio Carlos Jobim was arguably the most important composer of the 1960s bossa nova movement. The 1960s was an exciting decade for popular music with a wealth of pioneering talent in every genre: Bob Dylan was the original self-sufficient singer-songwriter; The Beatles revolutionized pop; Eric Clapton spearheaded the British Blues boom; and Jimi Hendrix made the guitar sound like it had never sounded before. There was also a revolution happening among writers. Composers (including Jobim and American songwriter Burt Bacharach) were writing very sophisticated songs with slick and unusual harmonic structures. Jobim's most famous tune, "The Girl from Ipanema", featured a middle section that was 16 bars long instead of eight, and modulated through no less than four tonal centres.

This solo guitar arrangement is an original tune inspired by the work of Antônio Carlos Jobim. The melody functions as a series of pick-up phrases that serve to anticipate each new chord change. In typical bossa nova style, the chord progression contains many non-diatonic chords, but never sounds disjointed or discordant.

Exercise
(Listen to track 45)

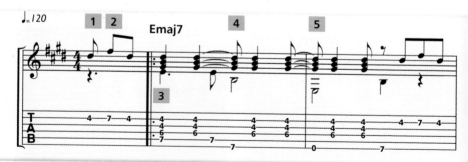

The chords you'll need for this lesson:

Pick the opening note of the tune with your first finger (i). It is perfectly acceptable to rest the thumb on the sixth string.

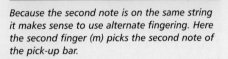

Because the second note is on the same string it makes sense to use alternate fingering. Here the second finger (m) picks the second note of the pick-up bar.

On the first beat of bar 1 the chord and bass note should be sounded together. Pick the notes using your thumb and fingers (i, m and a).

To play the low B bass note with the Emaj7 chord, move your fourth finger onto the sixth string. (Keep your other fingers in position to allow the chord to ring.)

The fourth finger can then be returned to its original position to allow the open sixth string to sound on the first beat of bar 2.

Am7	D9	C#7♭9	B7♭9	F7♭5	Emaj7
5fr.	4fr.	3fr.			7fr.

On the first beat of bar 3, the chord and bass note are sounded together. The strings are picked simultaneously using your thumb and fingers (i, m and a).

To allow the low open E to sound against the chord on the third beat, lift your second finger off the sixth string (but keep your first and second fingers in position).

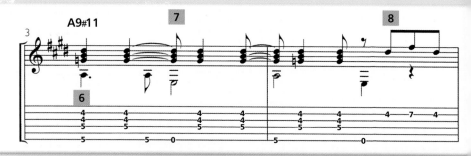

The melody notes at the end of bar 4 are fretted with your first and fourth fingers. Here, you can see the first finger fretting the D# with the fourth finger in position above the next note, F#.

The Emaj7 chord is played with a barre on the fourth fret using your first finger. The second finger can be angled to rest on top for extra strength as shown.

As you strike the sixth string with your thumb, your fingers (i, m and a) should be in position above their respective strings, ready to play the next chord.

As before, the melody notes at the end of this bar should be fretted with your first and fourth fingers. Here, you can see the F# on the seventh fret being played with the fourth finger.

The G#m7 chord is played by barring across the fourth fret with your first finger. Notice how the third finger is also in position, ready for the bass note on the third beat.

Top tip!
The secret to getting this arrangement to sound smooth and relaxed is in the organization of your fretting hand. Always make sure you're using the correct fingering by checking the photographs. Bad fingering = bad groove!

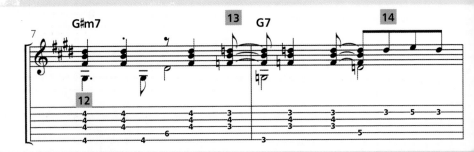

When you change to the G7 chord in bar 8, simply slide the barre chord down a fret and add your second finger on the third string.

Keep the first finger barre in place as you pick out the melody notes – this will enable you to play the chord change smoothly.

The F#m7 chord is identical to the shape used for G#m7 in bar 7; it's just played on the second fret instead of the fourth.

Because the following chord is no longer a full barre shape, the melody notes at the end of bar 10 are fretted individually. Here, you can see the first finger playing the C# on the second fret...

...and then the fourth finger playing the E on the fifth fret.

This Am7 chord is played with the second finger (sixth string) and third finger (barring across the second, third and fourth strings).

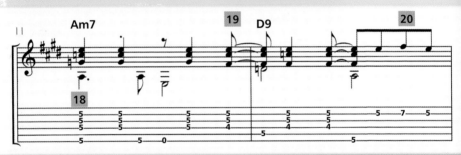

The change to the D9 chord should be a smooth motion that involves moving the second and third fingers (from Am7) one string higher. The first finger can then be added on the fifth string as shown.

Using your fourth finger, you should be able to play the melody notes at the end of bar 12 without releasing the D9 shape.

As you anticipate the C♯7♭9 chord at the end of bar 13, include the bass note on the fifth string (played with your second finger).

Add the low G♯ bass note in bar 14 by moving your second finger onto the sixth string. (The first and third fingers should remain in position throughout.)

Fret the melody notes at the end of this bar with your first and third fingers. Here you can see the D on the third fret being played with the first finger.

Play the B7♭9 chord at the beginning of bar 16 by barring across the first fret using your first finger. Be careful not to touch the fourth string with your second finger as you fret the bass note.

The melody notes at the end of this bar should be fretted with your first and third fingers. Here you can see the D♯ on the fourth fret being played with the first finger.

Top tip!
The bass part in this arrangement is slightly more intricate than the simple minim pattern demonstrated in lesson 26. Here, the root note is played as a dotted crotchet, followed by a quaver, before ascending or descending to the fifth. Listen to the CD and you'll recognize this as a familiar pattern that you'll have heard many times before.

Play the F7♭5 chord using your first finger (sixth string), second finger (fourth string) and third finger (third string). Ensure that the open second string is not inadvertently muted.

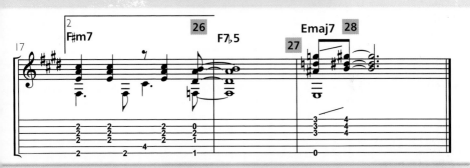

Play the penultimate chord (the chromatic approach to Emaj7) by simply barring across the third fret with your first finger…

…simply slide your finger up to the fourth fret (without re-picking the strings) for the final chord, Emaj7.

Lesson 28
Playing tenths

Learn how to identify and play the tenth interval, and how to use it to create some cool accompaniments.

The mysterious sounding tenth interval has been popular with guitarists and composers alike throughout the instrument's long history. From Mauro Giuliani's "Andante in C" (readers of a certain age will know this as the *Tales of the Riverbank* theme), which dates back to the early 19th century, to The Beatles' classic "Blackbird", tenths have been a mainstay of guitar-accompanying techniques for hundreds of years. Tenths are not the sole preserve of acoustic guitarists either; they also sound cool on electric. John Frusciante, of Red Hot Chili Peppers fame, has used them on many of the band's famous recordings, so much so that they have now become part of his trademark technique.

What is a tenth?
Major and minor thirds/tenths

A tenth, as its name suggests, is a note ten notes higher than the root note that is played with it. However, it has much more significance than that; it's the interval of a third played an octave higher. As you can see from the diagram above, double stop thirds are "close" intervals and can sound muddy when played in lower registers. When the third is played an octave higher (i.e., changing it from a "simple" to a "compound" interval), a much "wider" interval is created. The resulting double stop has a strong resonant quality on guitar, particularly when played with the root on the sixth string. Tenths can be used to play all of the diatonic chords in any major or minor key.

Exercise 1
(Listen to track 46)

This example illustrates how a classical guitarist might approach an arrangement by using tenths. The resulting chords are all diatonic to the key of G. Notice how the open D string is allowed to ring throughout.

The opening pinch should be played with your thumb (sixth string) and first finger (third string)...

...the thumb then moves across to strike the fourth string while the first two notes are allowed to ring on.

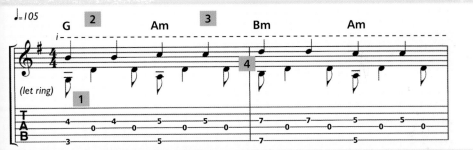

As you pick the third string on beat four, your thumb should be in position, ready to play the fourth string.

The opening pinch of bar 2 should also be picked with your thumb and first finger (i).

The G chord is fretted with just your first and third fingers. Make sure that your fingers don't inadvertently touch the fourth string and prevent it from sounding.

> **Top tip!**
> Tenths can be played with their lowest note on the sixth, fifth or fourth strings. Ideally, you should fret all tenths (both major and minor) using your second (low note) and third (high note) fretting hand fingers.

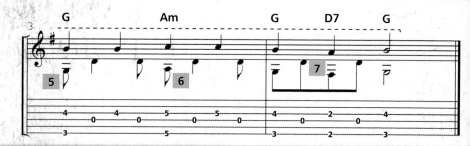

When you change to the Am chord on the third beat, keep your third finger on the third string and play the low A with your second finger.

The D7 chord in bar 4 should also be fretted with your second and third fingers (taking care not to mute the fourth string).

The Chili Peppers' guitar man extraordinaire John Frusciante defined the band's sound with his extensive use of tenths.

Exercise 2
(Listen to track 47)

Blues and jazz guitarists use tenths to create climbing lines that flesh out a simple underlying harmony. Here the technique is applied to the first two bars of a blues in E.

The opening hammer-on is played with your first finger (i). Here, you can see the first finger ready to play the slur as the third string is picked.

Pinch the ascending double stops with your thumb and first finger (i).

Here, you can see the last double stop in bar 1 as it should be fretted, using the second and third fingers.

The Beatles' song "Blackbird" is a great example of tenths in action. It involves the use of playing two strings at once, together with a healthy dose of time signature changes.

The double stop fingering changes slightly for the A7 chord. The low note is still played with the second finger, but the third finger (third string) is now a fret higher than the bass note…

…the shape then reverts to the previous shape (i.e., both fingers on the same fret) on the second beat.

Exercise 3
(Listen to track 48)

This example illustrates a more contemporary approach that could be used in a rock or pop ballad. You can use either your first (i) or second (m) picking hand fingers to play the notes on the second string.

Both melody and bass note should be fretted before you start picking the notes.

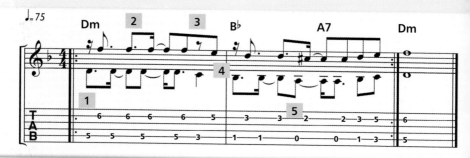

Here, the first finger (i) picks the melody note (F) on the second string.

As you move the chord down the fretboard, the chord shape changes. Here, the C chord is demonstrated with the first finger on the third fret and the third finger on the fifth fret.

The B♭ chord uses the same shape as the C chord (so you can slide the shape down in one movement); it's just located on the first fret.

The A7 chord only needs the second finger to play the C♯ on the second string, since the bass note is an open string.

Top tip!

Remember that when you're playing tenths primarily on one set of strings, you can always try including an open "drone" string as in exercise 1. This will dramatically change the texture of your accompaniment, and will sound cool on acoustic or electric guitar.

Lesson 29
Walking basslines

Learn how to jazz up your accompaniments with these cool walking basslines.

In the previous lesson you learned how to create climbing harmony using tenths. In this lesson you'll be looking at a less "dense" method of playing on every crotchet by adding a walking bassline to chords. Playing a bass note on every beat creates a groove that is described as "walking" because of the steady, regular momentum that it generates. Although walking bass is widely used in jazz, it can also be found in many other genres, as you'll see from the opposite list of well-known tunes.

How do I create walking basslines?

Walking basslines are created from a mixture of chord notes (arpeggios), scale notes and chromatic notes (notes from outside the scale). Since there are four beats in a bar, a three-note arpeggio is going to leave you a note short unless you repeat a note. This is where scale notes and chromatic notes come in handy. Scale notes can be used anywhere to create melodic basslines, but should be avoided on the first beat of the bar (where the harmony needs to be clearly outlined). Chromatic notes can be used to approach the next chord from a half step above or below, and link arpeggio and scale notes with chromatic passing notes.

Arpeggio plus chromatic note

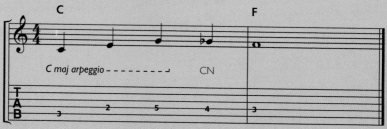

Famous walking basslines

Here are some songs where you can hear the walking bassline technique in action.

YES
"Yours Is No Disgrace"

RAY CHARLES
"Hit The Road Jack"

PEGGY LEE
"Fever"

MILES DAVIS
"Freddie Freeloader"

JIMI HENDRIX EXPERIENCE
"Hey Joe"

VAN MORRISON
"Moondance"

Adding chromatic notes between arpeggio and scale notes

Exercise 1
(Listen to track 49)
This example illustrates how to add a walking bassline to a blues sequence. Notice how just a simple two-note (double stop) chord is all that you need to create a full-sounding accompaniment.

The opening chord and bass note should be picked simultaneously using your thumb, first (i) and second (m) fingers.

Only the chord should be sounded on the off beat – play this using just your first (i) and second (m) fingers.

Play the descending G♭ bass note with your first finger. This will allow a smooth change to the F7 chord,...

...which should be fretted using your first finger (sixth string), second finger (fourth string) and third finger (third string).

The final C7 chord is fretted with just three fingers. Make sure that your second finger is not "leaning" onto the fourth string and preventing it from ringing.

Top tips!

• Remember that when you're playing walking basslines, you're creating the illusion of a bass player and guitarist playing together. Ideally the comping rhythms would be improvised, sometimes using short, percussive stabs, sometimes sustaining chords across several bass notes.

• Don't forget that only your thumb should play the bass notes. Chords should be picked with the first two or first three (i, m and a) fingers of your picking hand.

Exercise 2
(Listen to track 50)

Add a walking bassline to a one-chord vamp to create a driving groove. Let the second Am7 ring for its full value. Keep your fretting hand in position for as long as you can, then move to the third fret for the low G bass note.

Fret the Am7 chord with your second finger (sixth string) and third finger (forming a barre across the second, third and fourth strings).

By lifting your second finger off the string you can play the low open E bass note against the Am7 chord.

The G♯ bass note on the fourth beat should be fretted with your second finger. This will enable you to move quickly and smoothly to the Am7 chord.

Play the descending chromatic bassline in bar 2 entirely with your second finger. Here, you can see the second finger fretting the C on the eighth fret.

Exercise 3
(Listen to track 51)

The II–V–I sequence is common in many popular styles, including jazz and blues. Notice how the Dm7 (II) chord is restated on the fourth beat, just before the change to G7 (V) in the second bar.

The three-note Dm7 voicing should be fretted with the third finger (fifth string), first finger (fourth string) and fourth finger (third string).

Release the chord and move your first finger onto the fifth string to play the C bass note.

On the fourth beat the chord is re-picked with a low A bass note. Use the same fingering as in step 1 but move your third finger onto the sixth string.

The G7 chord should be fretted with your first finger (sixth string), second finger (fourth string) and third finger (third string).

Fret the Cmaj7 chord using your second finger (fifth string), first finger (fourth string) and third finger (third string).

CHAPTER 2

PICKING PATTERN DIRECTORY

This directory of picking patterns is intended as a useful "dip-in" reference section: a one-stop store for all your fingerpicking needs! Each pattern has been notated three ways: conventional, TAB and – unique to this book – an easy-to-understand "finger and string sequence" diagram. Having three different systems clearly outlines the three important elements (rhythm, fretting hand and picking hand positions) of each pattern. This will help you achieve quick results with the minimum of fuss. A brief description of each pattern's merits, specific technical demands and suggested uses, plus a recommended chord sequence to try it with, makes this section of the book truly different.

The picking patterns are in no particular order, so it's not necessary to work through them sequentially – unless you want to. And although typical genres are suggested for each pattern, this doesn't mean that the pattern can't be played in other styles. The patterns can, and should, be adapted to fit any kind of music, whether played on acoustic or electric guitar. Experiment by changing the feel or the tempo, or by omitting/adding notes. Think of these patterns as starting points that will help you create your own music… enjoy!

Picking pattern **No. 1**

This picking pattern is simple, but highly effective. It uses only three picking hand fingers (p, i and m) so it's easy to play. You'll find the pattern works well at both slow and fast tempos. Based on the early American folk style, its simple, repetitive form makes it ideal for self-accompaniment.

Suggested tempo range: 80–120 bpm

Finger and string sequence

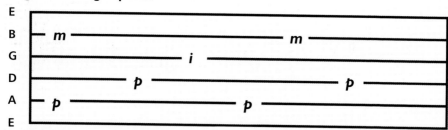

Try this pattern with this chord progression:

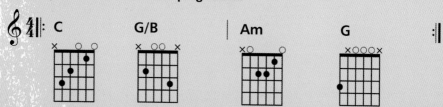

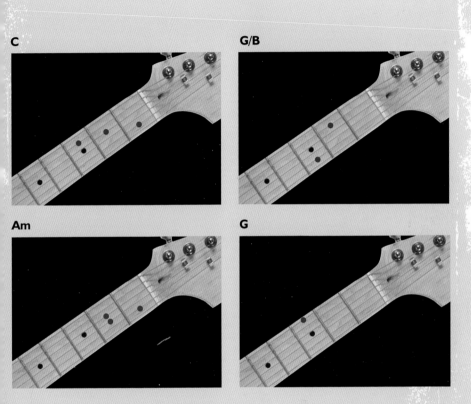

C

G/B

Am

G

Performance notes

When you apply the pattern to this sequence you'll need to change it slightly to accommodate the G chord with its sixth string root. Just pick the sixth string instead of the fifth (i.e., G instead of C) and play the rest of the pattern as before.

Picking pattern **No. 2**

This cool picking pattern works well with moveable chord shapes like the E7 shown; you can also use it with full barre chords, as in the suggested sequence below. With just a hint of a double-time groove, this pattern is perfect for blues, country and swamp rock genres.

Suggested tempo range: 80–100 bpm

Finger and string sequence

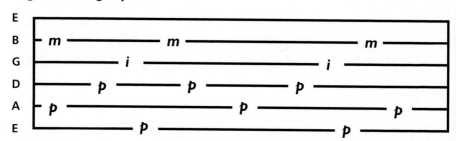

Try this pattern with this chord progression:

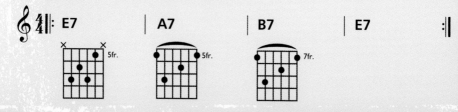

E7

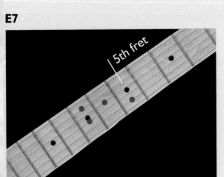

A7

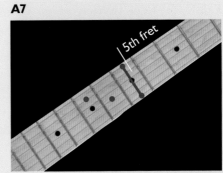

B7

Performance notes

Try playing this pattern with and without palm muting; it sounds great played both ways. To convert it to a six-string pattern, just reverse the first and third bass notes so you start on the root of the chord and not the fifth.

Picking pattern **No. 3**

Although this picking pattern uses all four of the picking hand fingers, the simple ascending sequence and lack of pinches make it easier to play than all those semiquavers might suggest! It's ideal for intros, outros or instrumental sections where a denser pattern is required – and perfect for slower classic rock tunes and ballads.

Suggested tempo range: 75–85 bpm

Finger and string sequence

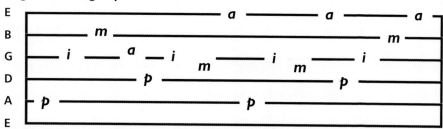

Try this pattern with this chord progression:

Am

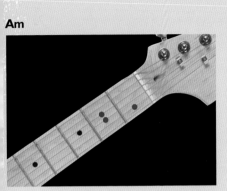

C

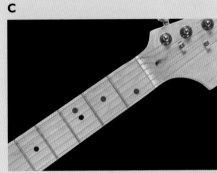

Dadd4

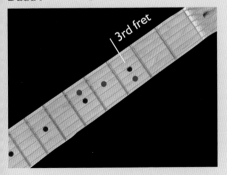

3rd fret

Performance notes

Because the top note of the chord is repeated on every beat, you can easily add melodies on the first string. Try alternating a high G (third fret) with the open E on the first string when you're picking out the Am and C chords.

Picking pattern **No. 4**

You may find this example a little tricky at first, but it's a cool pattern
that's well worth persevering with. Notice how the first note is
anticipated on repeats (the high G at the end of the fourth beat),
which creates a wonderfully hypnotic pattern. The driving bassline
also makes this an ideal singer-songwriter style self-accompaniment.

Suggested tempo range: 80–90 bpm

Finger and string sequence

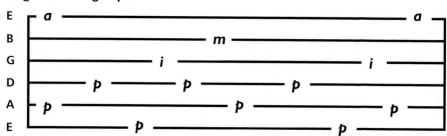

Try this pattern with this chord progression:

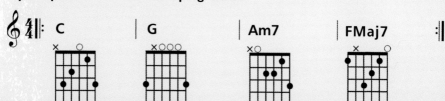

C

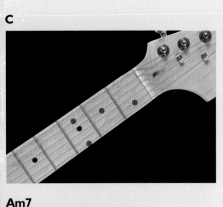

G

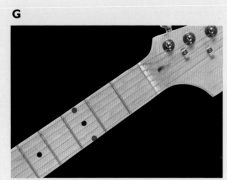

Am7

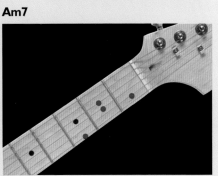

FMaj7

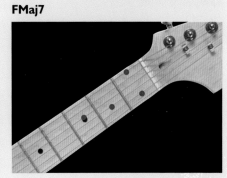

Performance notes

The high G remains the top voice for the first three chords; it can also be alternated with the open E. Fret the root note of the Fmaj7 chord with your thumb on the sixth string.

Picking pattern **No. 5**

This double-time-feel example should be played with swing semiquavers. The bass notes should also be palm muted to avoid overpowering the melody notes, creating a more percussive and rhythmic accompaniment. This is an ideal pattern for creating authentic blues arrangements.

Suggested tempo range: 60–70 bpm

Finger and string sequence

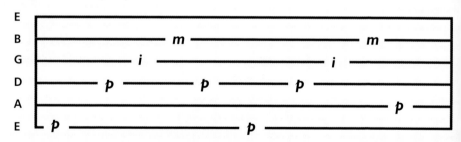

Try this pattern with this chord progression:

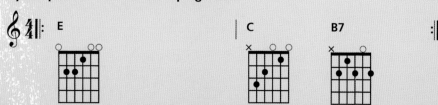

E

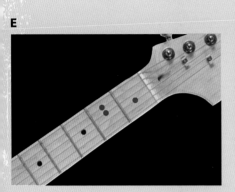

C

B7

Performance notes

When you play the C and B7 chords, the lowest bass note falls on the fifth string. Just adapt the bass picking so that the bass notes are played on the fifth and fourth strings (with the root on the fifth).

Picking pattern **No. 6**

A grooving double-time-feel pattern with swing semiquavers that's ideal for electric or acoustic blues arrangements. The example incorporates a powerful alternating bassline (using octaves) to generate a real sense of motion. Palm muting is essential for taming those bass notes!

Suggested tempo range: 80–120 bpm

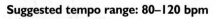

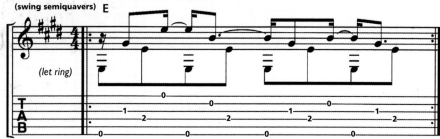

Finger and string sequence

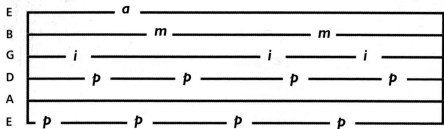

Try this pattern with this chord progression:

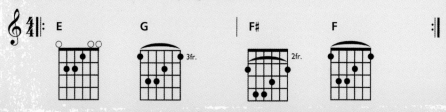

E

G

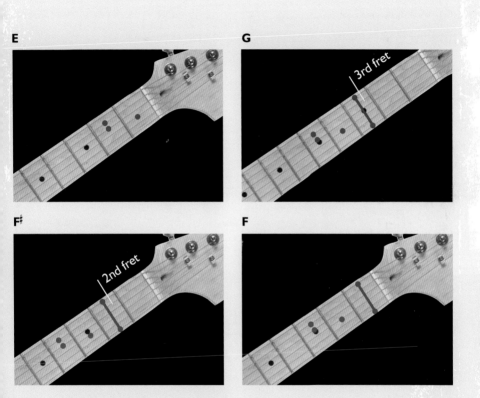

F#

F

Performance notes

This sequence could be used as the main
section of an arrangement (i.e., with repeats),
or as a turnaround at the end of a 12-bar
blues sequence. The pattern remains the
same, whether played with full barre chords
or open shapes.

Picking pattern **No. 7**

This is a more percussive, contemporary style of accompaniment that works well with pop and rock styles. Just hit the strings with your picking fingers (while still holding down the chord shape) on beats two and four. This emphasizes the backbeat (where the snare drum usually falls) and creates a wonderfully rhythmic groove.

Suggested tempo range: 95–115 bpm

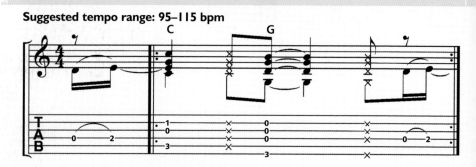

Finger and string sequence

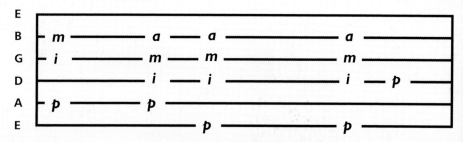

Try this pattern with this chord progression:

C

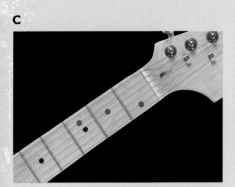

G

F

Performance notes

The hammered-on bass note in the pick-up bar (and at the end of the sequence before repeating) should be allowed to ring into the first chord. When hitting the strings with your fingers, allow them to remain on the strings momentarily. This keeps the strings from ringing (thus preventing unwanted harmonics).

Picking pattern **No. 8**

This cool picking pattern can be played with just the thumb and index finger of your picking hand! It's a pop/rock pattern that conjures up a 1960s vibe, particularly when teamed with the descending chord sequence suggested below. This pattern sounds great on electric or acoustic guitar.

Suggested tempo range: 80–90 bpm

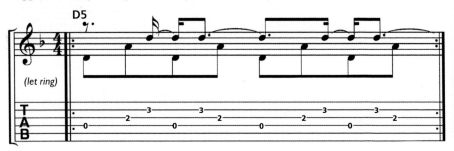

Finger and string sequence

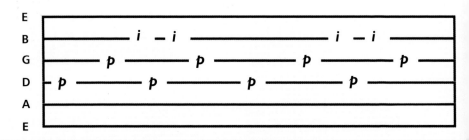

Try this pattern with this chord progression:

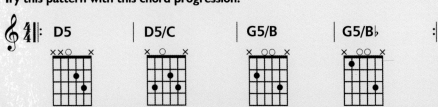

D5

D5/C

G5/B

G5/B♭

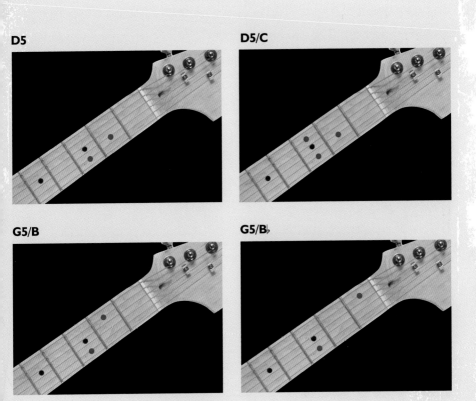

Performance notes

This pattern spans just three strings when played with the D5 chord. All of the remaining chords have their lowest note on the fifth string, so start the pattern on the fifth instead of the fourth string, but keep the rest of the pattern just as before.

Picking pattern **No. 9**

A pop pattern with a country flavour, this accompaniment has a pinch on beats one and three. The recurring pinches establish a hypnotic melodic fragment that can be continued through an entire sequence, as shown. The hint of a double-time feel provided by the alternating bass part prevents slower tempo tunes from becoming boring.

Suggested tempo range: 65–75 bpm

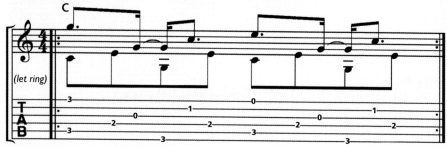

Finger and string sequence

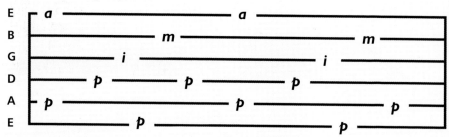

Try this pattern with this chord progression:

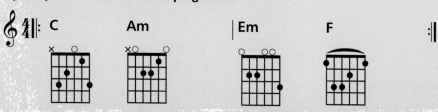

C

Am

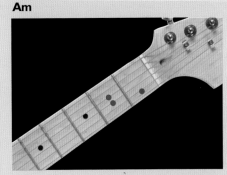

Em

F

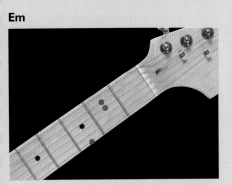

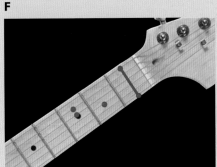

Performance notes

Remember that you can always add melody notes to chords – don't stick religously to the same old shapes! By adding a high G on the first string to the Em shape in this sequence, the melody established in the first bar can be repeated in the second, but over different chords. This is an extremely effective technique to use in your accompaniments.

Picking pattern **No. 10**

This classic country-style pattern has its roots in bluegrass mountain music. The unusual pinch on the first off beat sets up a cool syncopated melody part that, although a little tricky rhythmically, only uses the first two fingers (i and m) of your picking hand. With its double-time feel, this pattern sounds impressive at faster tempos.

Suggested tempo range: 80–120 bpm

(let ring)

Finger and string sequence

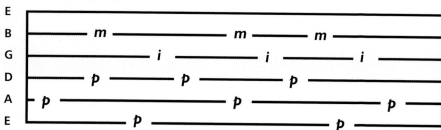

Try this pattern with this chord progression:

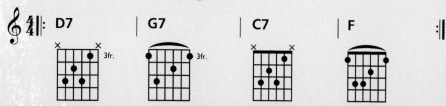

D7

G7

C7

F

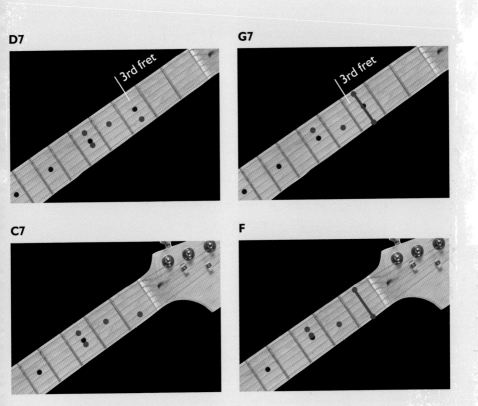

Performance notes

This is an easy pattern to transfer from a five-string root chord to a six-string root chord (i.e., G7 and F). Don't change the strings your fingers pick; just modify the bass pattern by starting on the sixth and alternating the fourth string with the fifth. In other words, the string pattern for D7 and C7 should be: 5–4–6–4; for G7 and for F it changes to: 6–4–5–4.

Picking pattern **No. 11**

A wonderful jangly picking pattern that's perfect for slow, groovin' rock tunes. This will work well on acoustic, but comes into its own on electric, where a dash of chorus and reverb will really bring this pattern to life. This accompaniment works best when played at slower tempos.

Suggested tempo range: 70–80 bpm

Finger and string sequence

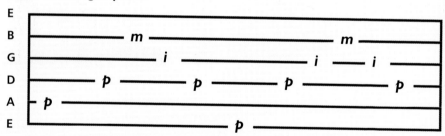

Try this pattern with this chord progression:

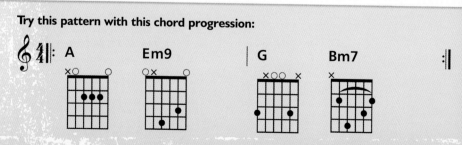

A

Em9

G

Bm7

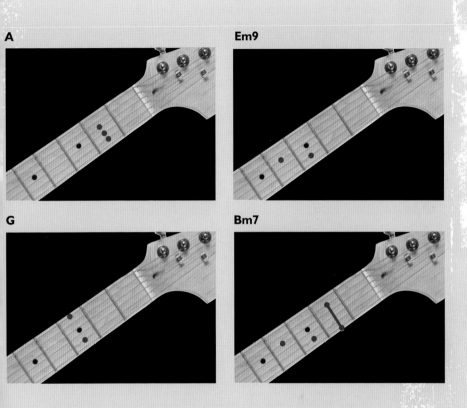

Performance notes

For this part to work effectively, it's important
to allow the strings to ring into each other.
Make sure when you're fretting the Em9 chord
that you don't inadvertently damp the open
third string when you're fretting the fourth.

Picking pattern **No. 12**

This is the perfect pattern for ballads and slower tunes. The hammer-on adds a touch of sophistication without over-complicating the part, making it the perfect accompaniment for the solo singer-songwriter. It could also provide an ideal interlude or verse section in a full band scenario, where contrast and space are needed.

Suggested tempo range: 75–85 bpm

Finger and string sequence

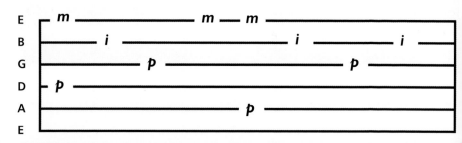

Try this pattern with this chord progression:

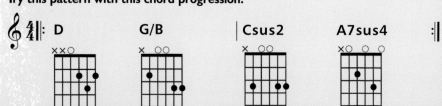

D

G/B

Csus2

A7sus4

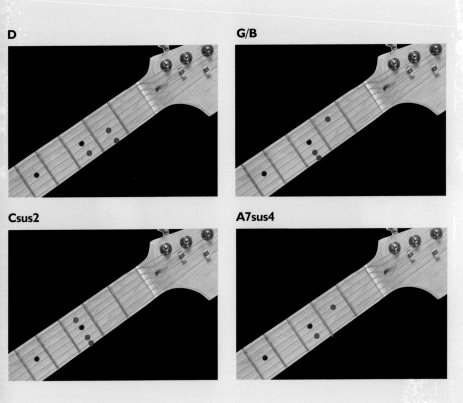

Performance notes

In the second bar, the hammer-on can be omitted on the Csus2 chord. Use the same picking pattern as above, but start on the fifth string instead of the fourth. Allow all the notes to ring into each other, for maximum effect.

Picking pattern **No. 13**

The combination of alternating bass notes and a syncopated, repeated melodic pattern makes this the perfect choice for self-accompaniments. It suits many styles from 1960s folk to country, and even classic rock. Notice how all the melody notes fall on the off beats between the bass notes, creating a rich tapestry of cascading notes.

Suggested tempo range: 90–100 bpm

Finger and string sequence

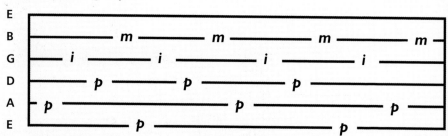

Try this pattern with this chord progression:

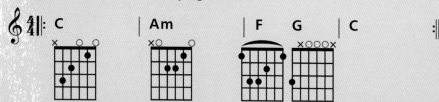

C

Am

F

G

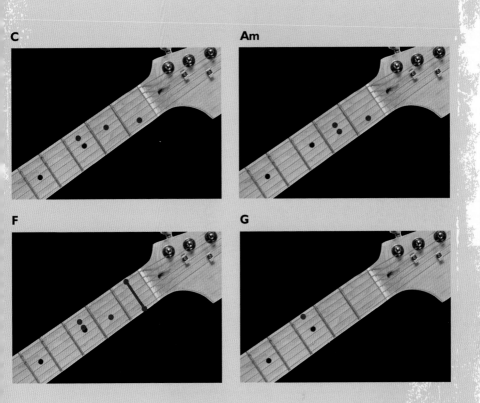

Performance notes

When you change to the sixth-string root chords F and G, you can adapt the bass part so that it becomes a simple alternating pattern on the sixth and fourth strings. The melody should remain constant with no string changes.

Picking pattern **No. 14**

This dominant, pedal-based (i.e., where the V chord/root chord is repeatedly played) pattern would be ideal as an intro/interlude section. Alternatively, it can be used in the sequence below to form a complete verse or chorus section. It's not genre specific; the G7sus4 chord gives the pattern a contemporary feel, but it would work well in any style.

Suggested tempo range: 75–85 bpm

Finger and string sequence

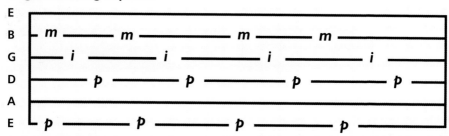

Try this pattern with this chord progression:

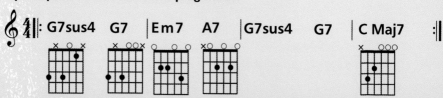

G7sus4

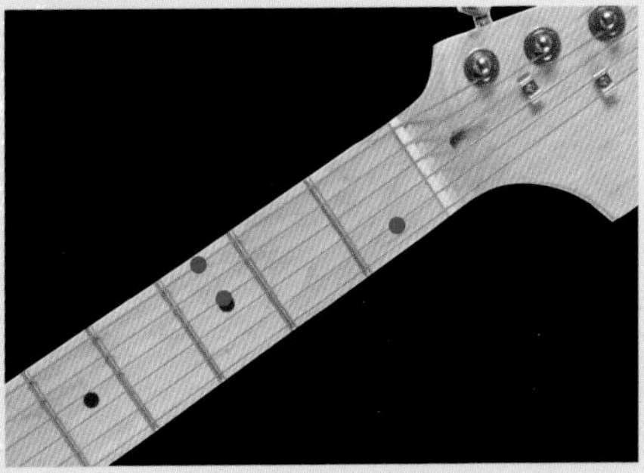

G7

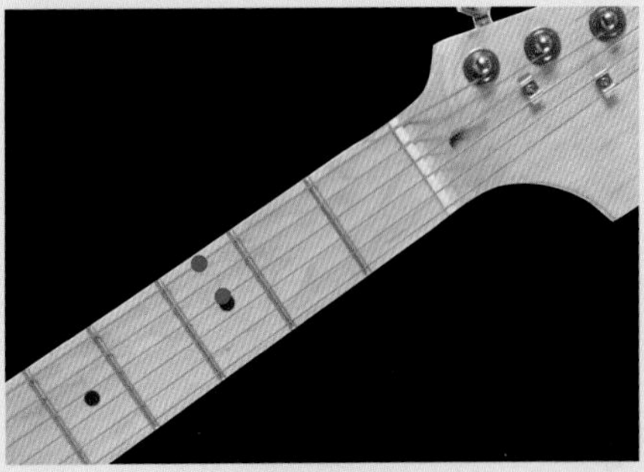

Em7

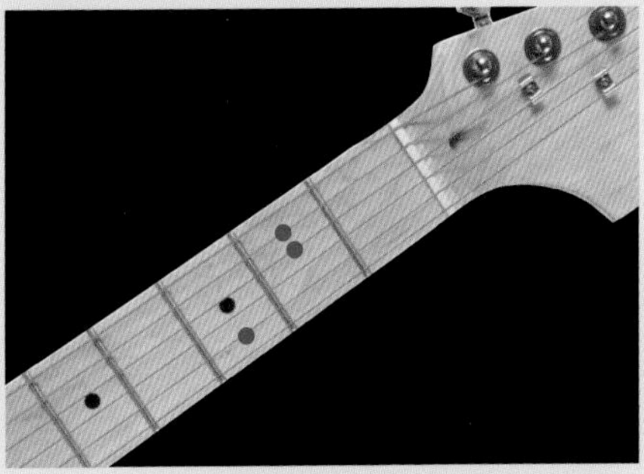

A7

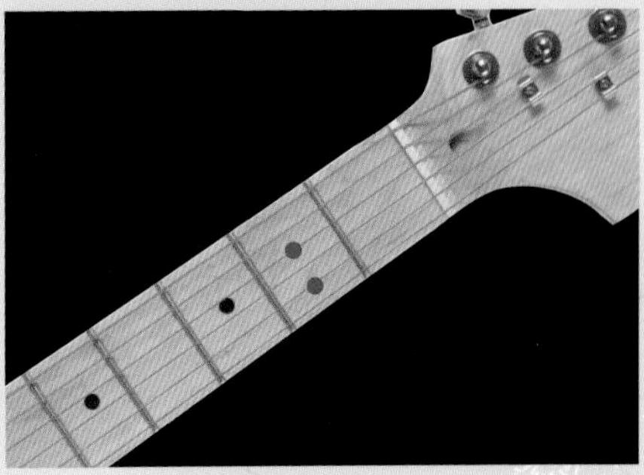

Cmaj7

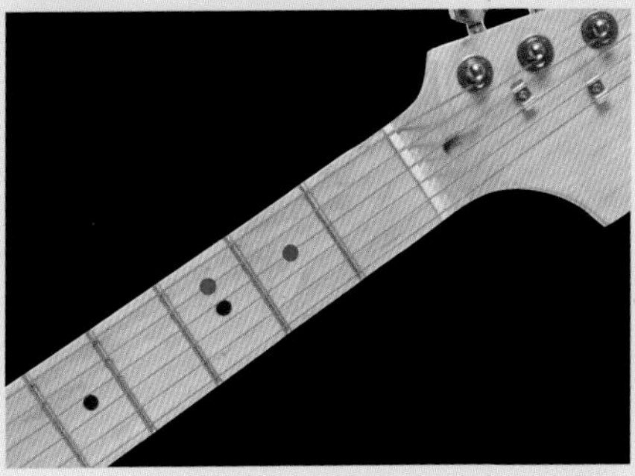

Performance notes

Although this pattern looks quite complex, after a little practice you'll find that it's quite straightforward. You'll need to adapt the pattern slightly for the A7 and Cmaj7 chords with their fifth-string roots. Move the lowest bass note onto the fifth string and keep the upper note on the fourth, as in the original.

Picking pattern **No. 15**

This haunting, sparse, yet full-sounding pattern is ideal for contemporary acoustic or electric blues accompaniments. The melody notes sit comfortably against the relentless quaver bassline, creating an unusual but highly effective pattern. The high E at the end of the pattern should be allowed to ring into successive repeats.

Suggested tempo range: 70–80 bpm

Finger and string sequence

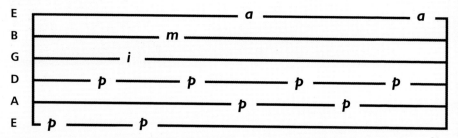

Try this pattern with this chord progression:

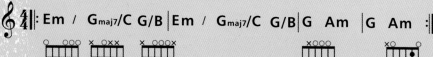

Em

Gmaj7/C

G/B

G

Am

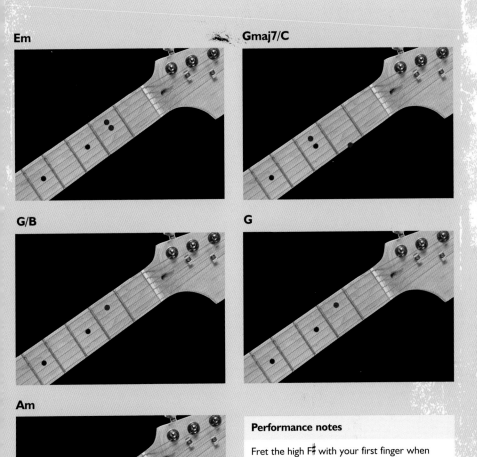

Performance notes

Fret the high F♯ with your first finger when playing the Gmaj7/C chord. You can then use your second finger to fret both notes on the fifth string (while allowing the F♯ to ring for its full value). At the end of the third bar, try anticipating the high G (first string) of the following G chord.

Picking pattern **No. 16**

This cool rock 'n' roll riff is a driving groove that works just as well in Southern swing-style country. Keeping the bass notes on the beat while playing syncopated chords "in the gaps" creates the mojo here. The off-beat semiquaver chords are played with a shuffle feel. If you're doing it right, it'll feel as though the chords are tumbling into the bass notes.

Suggested tempo range: 110–120 bpm

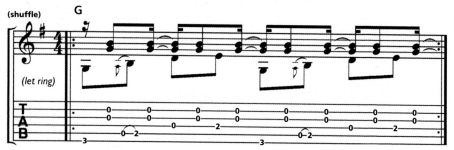

Finger and string sequence

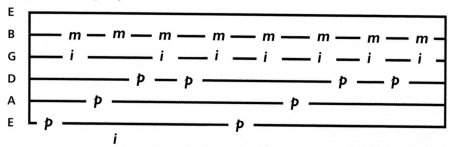

Try this pattern with this chord progression:

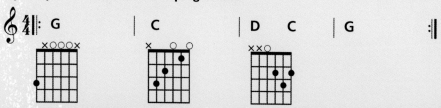

G

C

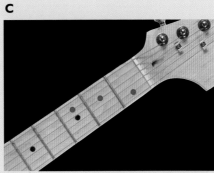

D

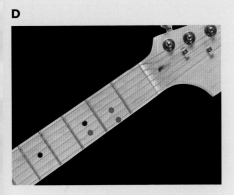

Performance notes

By now you should have no problem adapting riffs to fit different chord shapes. Always think about the intervals that make up the riff, and how it should sound. Then just get transposing – the more you do this, the quicker you'll get. Try playing the D chord by barring across the second fret with your first finger. This will leave your third finger free for adding the riff notes.

Picking pattern **No. 17**

A versatile picking pattern with a strong country flavour, this example is ideal for up-tempo and double-time grooves. Notice how the thumb moves onto the third string while the fingers (i and m) pick out a constant, syncopated rhythm. At faster tempos the pattern starts to resemble a traditional banjo roll.

Suggested tempo range: 90–120 bpm

Finger and string sequence

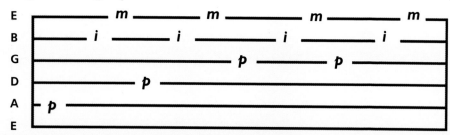

Try this pattern with this chord progression:

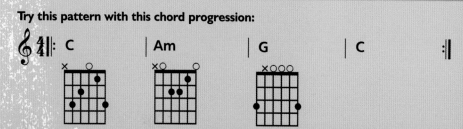

Picking pattern **No. 18**

This singer-songwriter accompaniment pattern works well with "two chords per bar" sequences, as in the suggested progression shown. Only the first melody note is pinched; the remainder are all syncopated. For the best results, start slowly and build to the suggested tempo range gradually.

Suggested tempo range: 80–100 bpm

Finger and string sequence

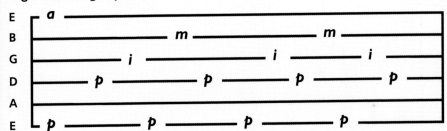

Try this pattern with this chord progression:

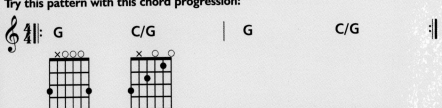

Picking pattern **No. 19**

This is a dark and moody fingerstyle riff that's ideal for acoustic or electric blues accompaniments. Although the bassline incorporates the minor third (B♭), the chord voicing omits the third (hence the G5 symbol). This makes it ideal for creating harmonically ambiguous accompaniments – perfect for all blues styles.

Suggested tempo range: 70–80 bpm

Finger and string sequence

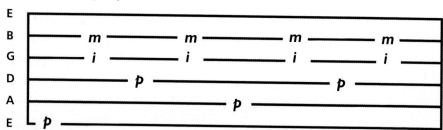

Try this pattern with this chord progression:

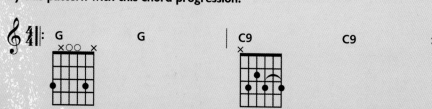

Picking pattern **No. 20**

A beautiful cascading, hypnotic pattern that works really well with pop or country ballads. This pattern can be played with five- or six-string chord shapes, but doesn't transfer well to four-string shapes; hence the D9/F♯ instead of D7 in the suggested sequence below.

Suggested tempo range: 75–85 bpm

Finger and string sequence

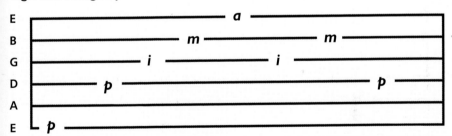

Try this pattern with this chord progression:

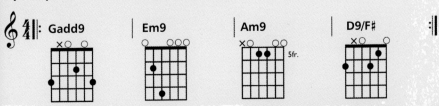

Picking pattern **No. 21**

This classic pop/rock ballad style accompaniment creates a rich harmonic backdrop by sounding high fretted notes against open strings. There are many other open chord fragments that can be played against open strings – experiment by moving them around the neck to find the positions that work best.

Suggested tempo range: 70–80 bpm

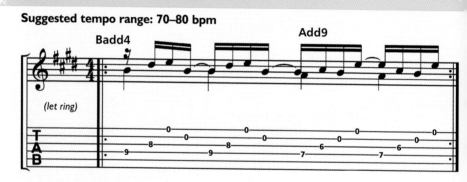

Finger and string sequence

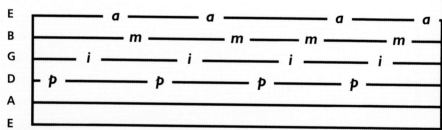

Try this pattern with this chord progression:

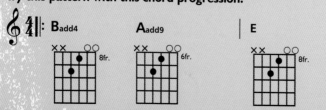

Picking pattern **No. 22**

This picking pattern works extremely well in pop/rock style ballads. It incorporates hammer-ons and pull-offs to create a sophisticated, fluid accompaniment. The pattern can be adapted to work with moveable shapes, but without the HO/PO ornamentation.

Suggested tempo range: 80–120 bpm

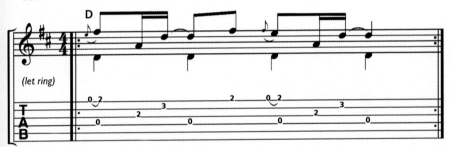

Finger and string sequence

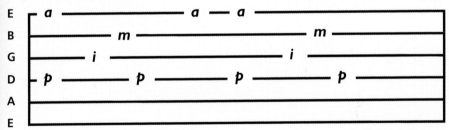

Try this pattern with this chord progression:

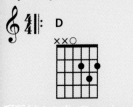

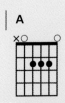

Picking pattern **No. 23**

This chiming pop ballad-style pattern generates a real sense of space without sacrificing the groove. It sounds great on electric or acoustic, and is ideal for intros and verse sequences where a lighter accompaniment is required.

Suggested tempo range: 75–85 bpm

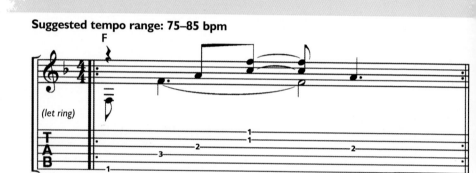

Finger and string sequence

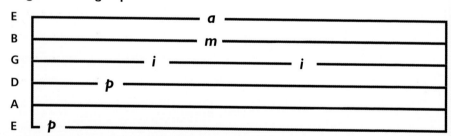

Try this pattern with this chord progression:

Picking pattern **No. 24**

This pattern is perfect for funky blues-flavoured accompaniments.
The lack of a shuffle (swing) feel gives the pattern a more
contemporary sound and makes it ideal for a wide variety of
accompaniment scenarios. This pattern works equally well on
either electric or acoustic guitar.

Suggested tempo range: 70–80 bpm

Finger and string sequence

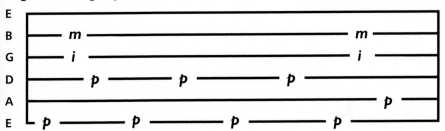

Try this pattern with this chord progression:

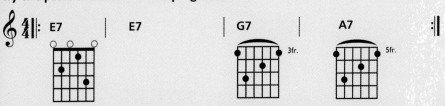

Picking pattern **No. 25**

This pattern is perfect for playing a swinging minor blues, jazz standard or even a pop tune with a swing feel. It works well with either open or moveable shapes (the hammer-on should be omitted when using the latter). Sounds very cool at fast tempos when playing in jazzier styles.

Suggested tempo range: 120–140 bpm

Finger and string sequence

Try this pattern with this chord progression:

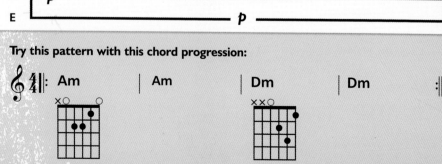

Picking pattern **No. 26**

This pattern is perfect for 12/8 ballads and works well in a wide range of genres. The classic ascend/descend picking pattern provides an interesting accompaniment without ever becoming too intrusive.

Suggested tempo range: 55–65 bpm

Finger and string sequence

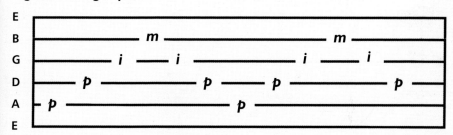

Try this pattern with this chord progression:

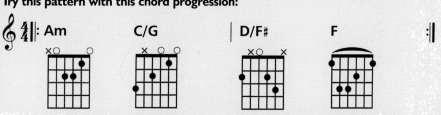

Picking pattern **No. 27**

This sparse but interesting pattern creates a beautiful hypnotic accompaniment that works in many different rock styles. It's perfect for creating spacey interludes or verse sections. It would sound equally at home in a classic rock tune with a belting chorus, or in a dark and moody contemporary arrangement with dropped tuning.

Suggested tempo range: 70–80 bpm

Finger and string sequence

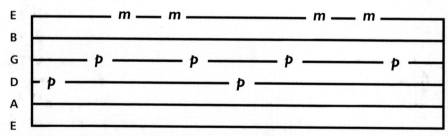

Try this pattern with this chord progression:

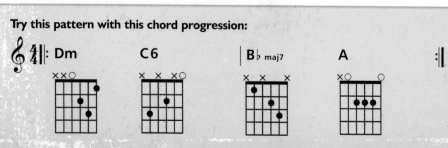

Picking pattern **No. 28**

An ideal self-accompaniment in the classic acoustic singer-songwriter style, this pattern creates interest and a sense of motion by adding a melody on the first string. The pattern itself is very straightforward, with only the upper pinched note changing on the third beat. It's an easy way to add a touch of class to any picking pattern.

Suggested tempo range: 70–85 bpm

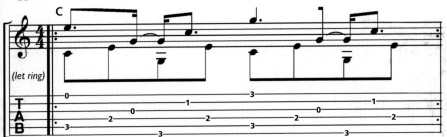

Finger and string sequence

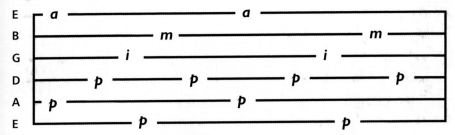

Try this pattern with this chord progression:

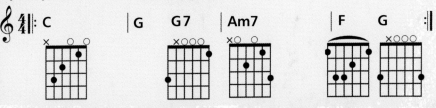

Picking pattern **No. 29**

This prog rock-flavoured accompaniment is ideal for intros, outros or contrasting interlude sections. The ascending double stops (pinches) create a spacey floating backdrop that could be intensified on a 12-string guitar. Effective on acoustic or electric, this pattern is better suited to slower songs and ballads.

Suggested tempo range: 70–80 bpm

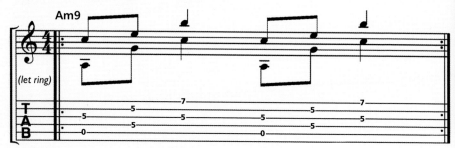

Finger and string sequence

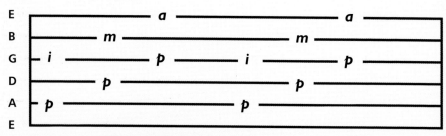

Try this pattern with this chord progression:

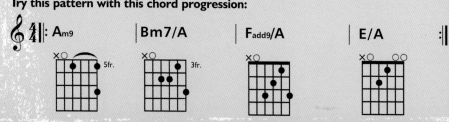

Picking pattern **No. 30**

This is an extremely simple but highly effective accompaniment in 3/4 time. With its "loping" feel and a hint of 6/8, this pattern can easily sustain a driving groove through any song. It's perfect for traditional folk or country ballads, but would work well in other genres too. Three-time ballad grooves are usually played at brisker tempos.

Suggested tempo range: 110–120 bpm

Finger and string sequence

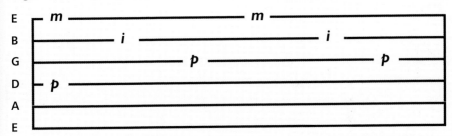

Try this pattern with this chord progression:

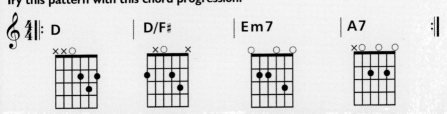

CHAPTER 3

CAPO KEYS

By using a capo, a picking pattern can be transposed without having to change chord shapes. Why would you need to do this? Well, first to find the best key for a singer's voice (or your own if you're self-accompanying), and second to create new sounds. A capo changes the timbre of the guitar: the higher the capo, the "tighter" the sound. This can be useful in a recording situation where a second guitar part is often added to "fatten" the sound.

Here you'll find which keys are available on any given fret. You'll also be able to find alternative locations for the same key using a different set of open chords. For instance, the sequence C–F–G7 could be played with the capo on the third fret, the fifth fret or the tenth fret. Each capo position has its own unique sound, and enables slurs and ornamentations to be added, not otherwise possible.

Five major and two minor keys are given for each capo position up to the ninth fret (this is the last playable position on a non-cutaway guitar). Chords I–IV–V are stated for each key (with V being a dominant seventh). Remember, it's not always necessary to fret all of the chord notes, and sixth-string root chords can also be played using the fretting hand thumb.

Indicates fret location of capo

Indicates effective open chord region

Indicates new "virtual" third fret (i.e., location of root for C and G chord shapes)

Capo keys:
first fret keys

Key	Chord shapes

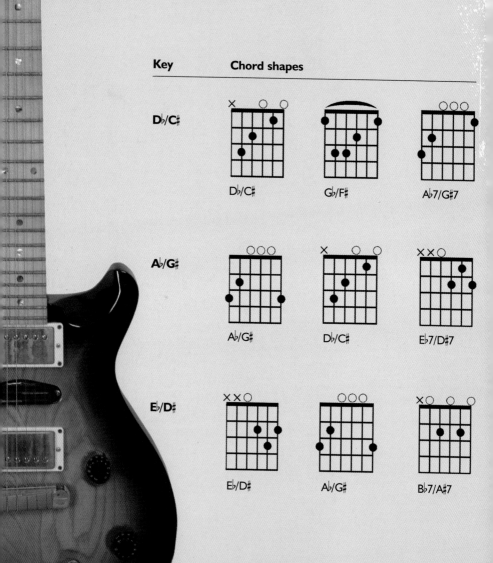

D♭/C♯

D♭/C♯   G♭/F♯   A♭7/G♯7

A♭/G♯

A♭/G♯   D♭/C♯   E♭7/D♯7

E♭/D♯

E♭/D♯   A♭/G♯   B♭7/A♯7

Key	Chord shapes

B♭/A♯

B♭/A♯   E♭/D♯   F7

F

F   B♭/A♯   C7

B♭ minor

B♭m   E♭m   F7

F minor

Fm   B♭m   C7

Capo keys:
second fret keys

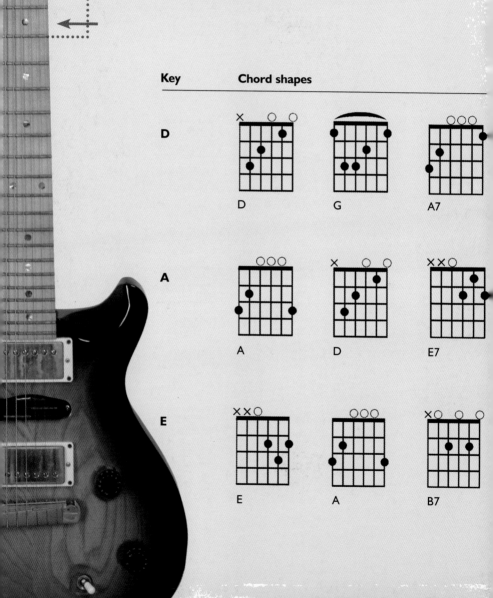

Key	Chord shapes		
D	D	G	A7
A	A	D	E7
E	E	A	B7

Key	Chord shapes		

B

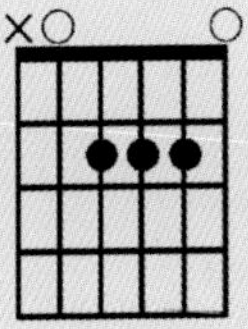

B 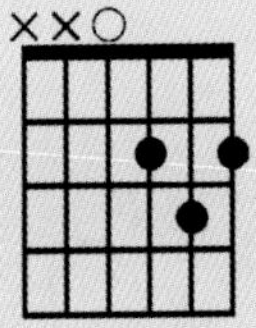   E 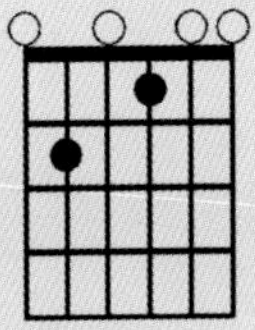   F#7

F#

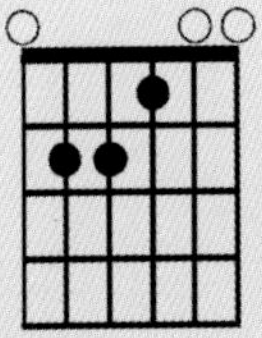

F# 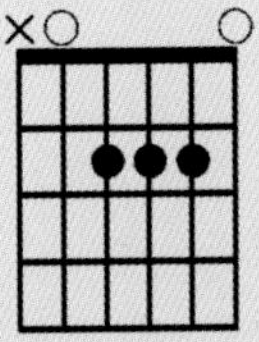   B 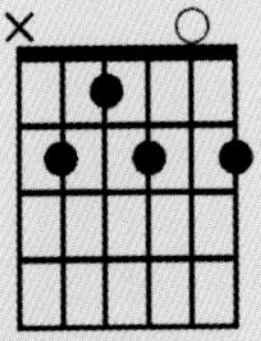   C#7

B minor

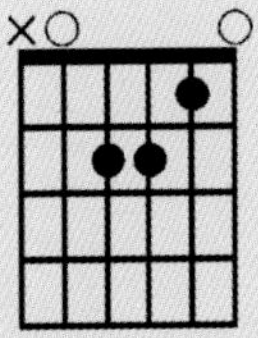

Bm 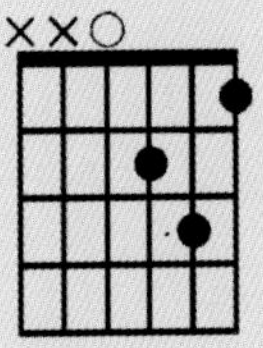   Em 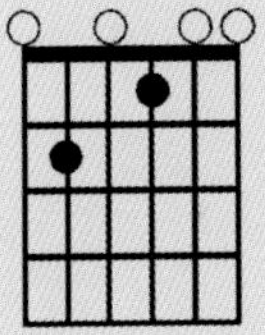   F#7

F# minor

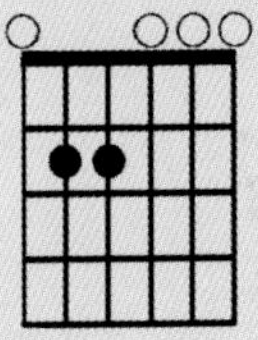

F#m 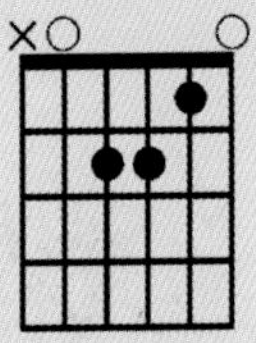   Bm 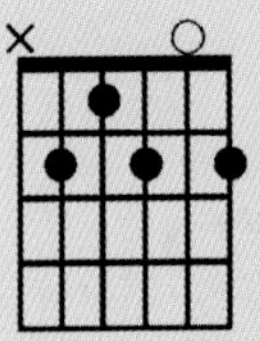   C#7

Capo keys:
third fret keys

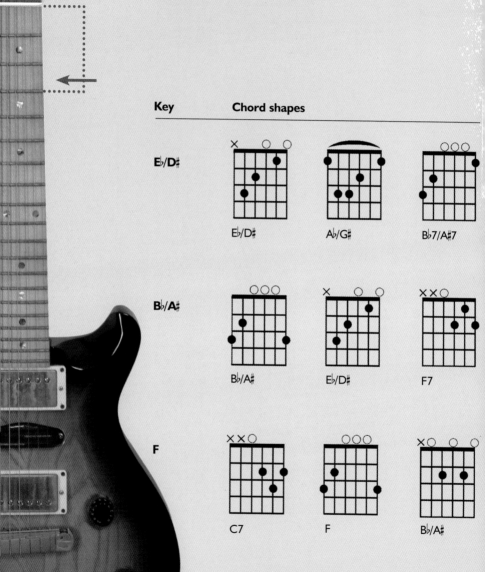

Key	Chord shapes		
Eb/D#	Eb/D#	Ab/G#	Bb7/A#7
Bb/A#	Bb/A#	Eb/D#	F7
F	C7	F	Bb/A#

Key	Chord shapes

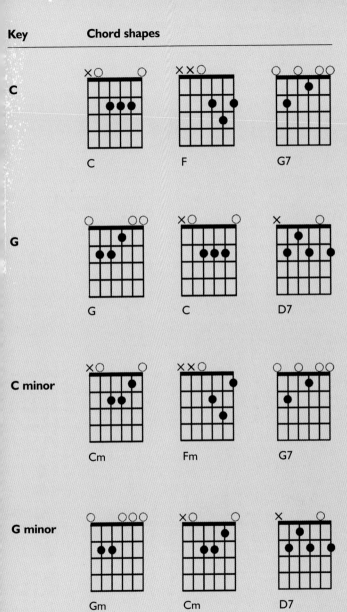

C

C   F   G7

G

G   C   D7

C minor

Cm   Fm   G7

G minor

Gm   Cm   D7

Capo keys:
fourth fret keys

Key	Chord shapes

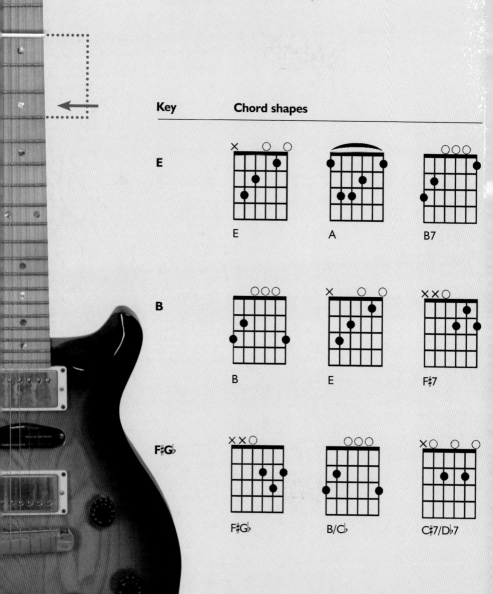

E

E   A   B7

B

B   E   F#7

F#/G♭

F#/G♭   B/C♭   C#7/D♭7

Key	Chord shapes

C♯/D♭

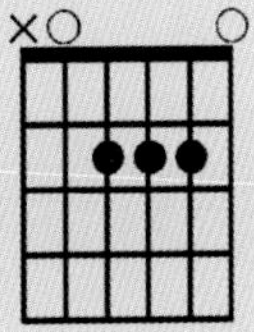

C♯/D♭ 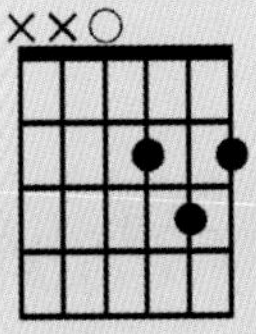 F♯/G♭ 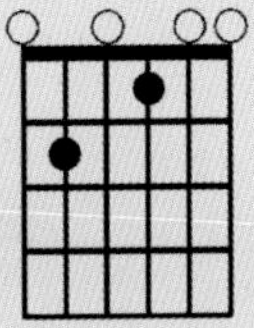 G♯7/A♭7

G♯/A♭

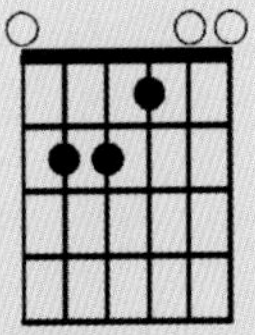

G♯/A♭ 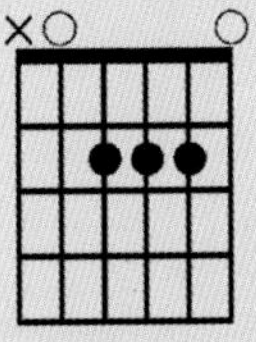 C♯/D♭ 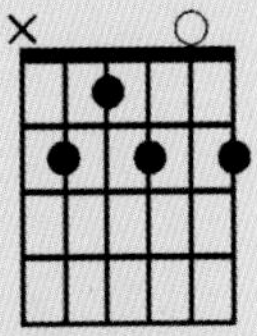 D♯7/E♭7

C♯/D♭ minor

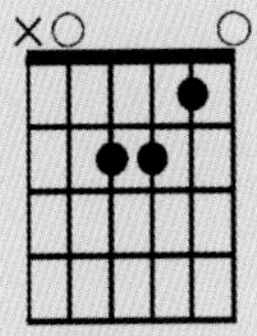

C♯/D♭m 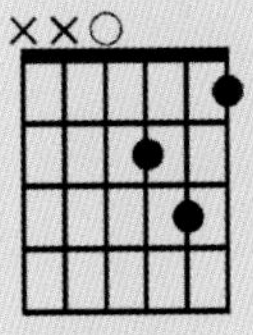 F♯/G♭m 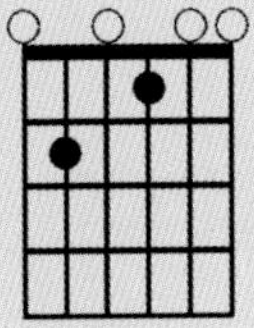 G♯/A♭7

G♯/A♭ minor

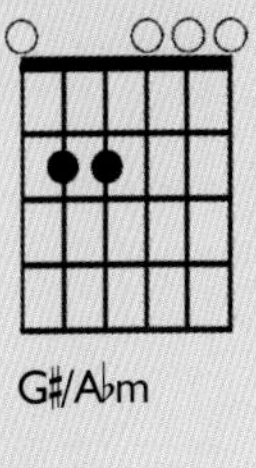

G♯/A♭m 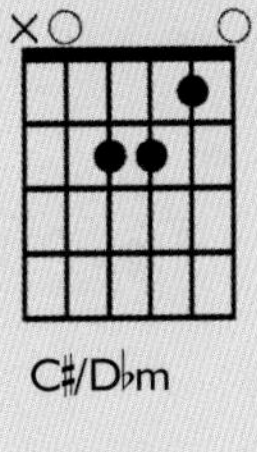 C♯/D♭m 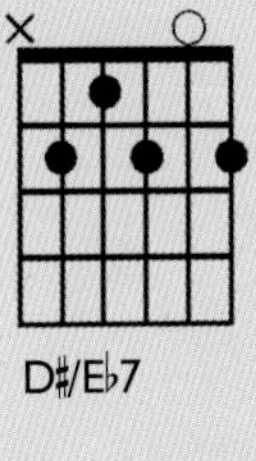 D♯/E♭7

Capo keys:
fifth fret keys

Key	Chord shapes		

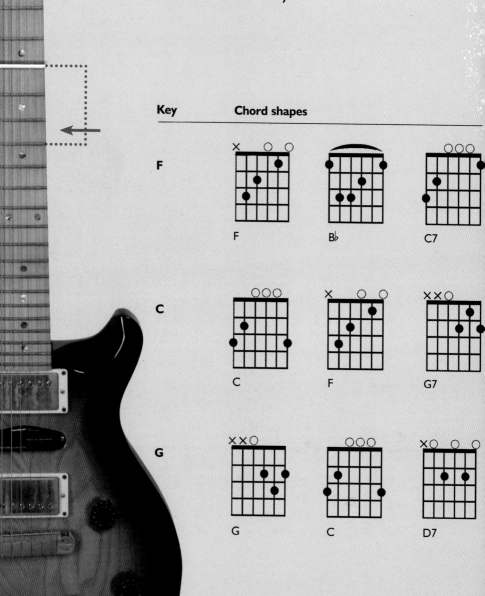

F

F   Bb   C7

C

C   F   G7

G

G   C   D7

Key	Chord shapes

D

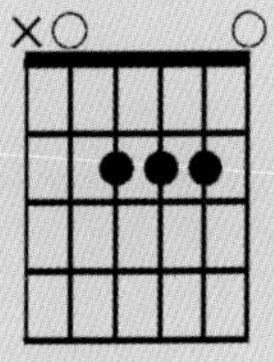

D 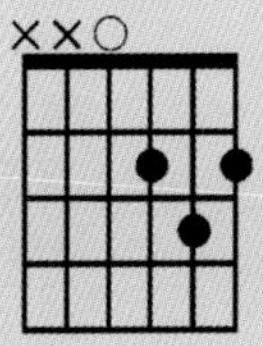 G 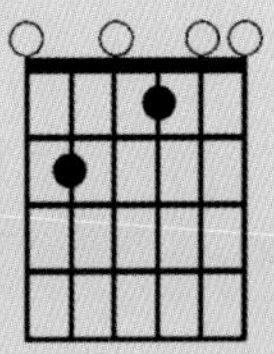 A7

A

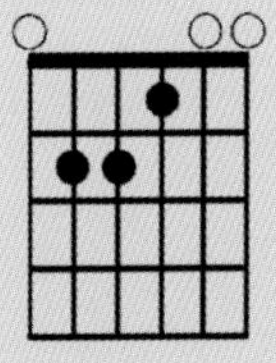

A 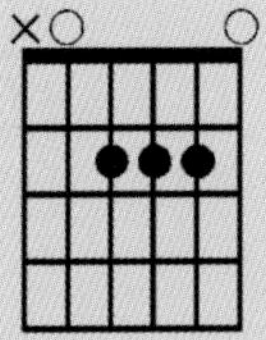 D 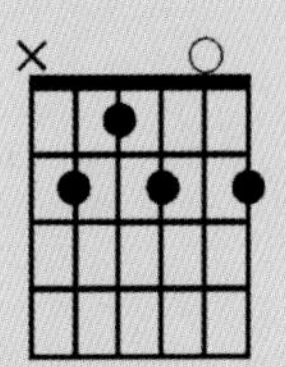 E7

D minor

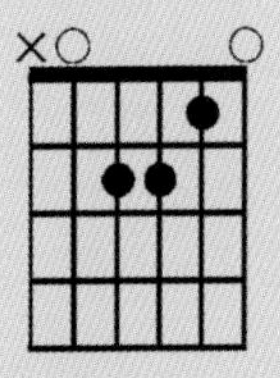

Dm 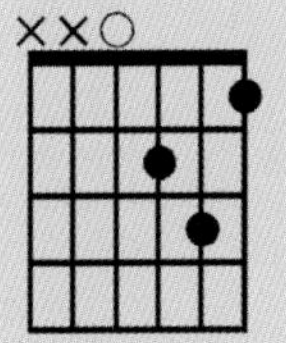 Gm 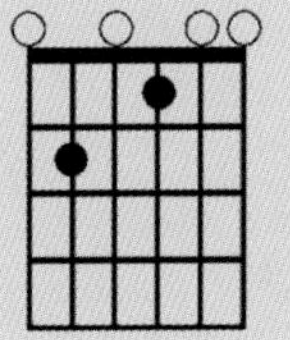 A7

A minor

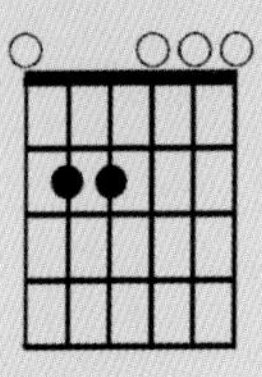

Am 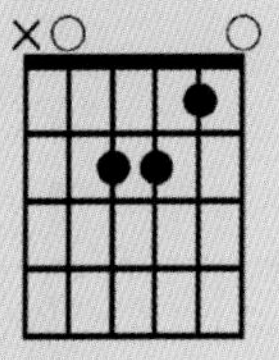 Dm 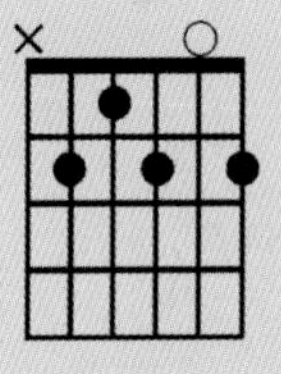 E7

Capo keys:
sixth fret keys

Key	Chord shapes

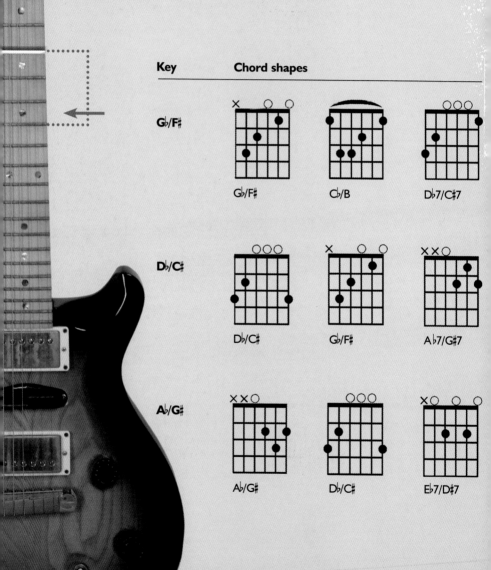

Gb/F#

Gb/F#   Cb/B   Db7/C#7

Db/C#

Db/C#   Gb/F#   Ab7/G#7

Ab/G#

Ab/G#   Db/C#   Eb7/D#7

Key	Chord shapes		

E♭/D♯

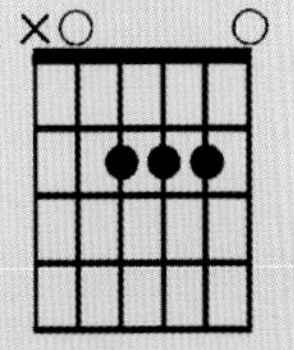

E♭/D♯   A♭/G♯   B♭7/A♯7

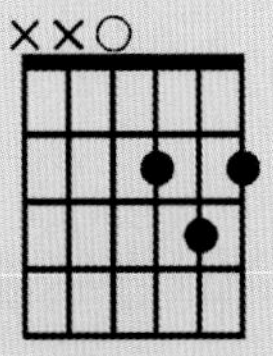

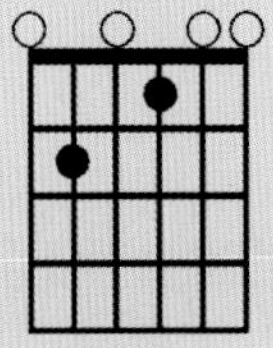

B♭/A♯

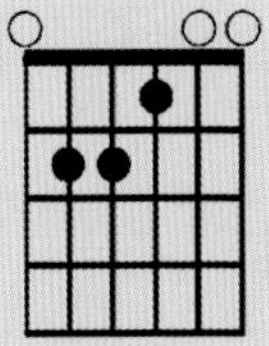

B♭/A♯   E♭/D♯   F7/E♯7

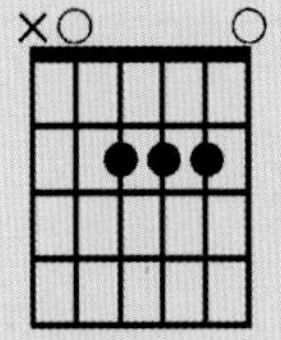

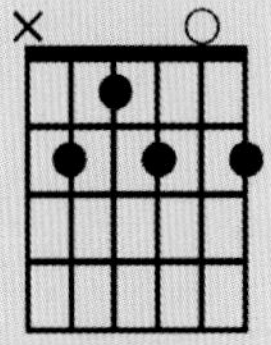

E♭/D♯ minor

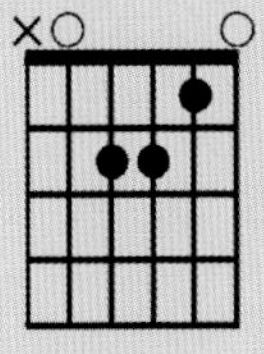

E♭/D♯m   A♭/G♯m   B♭7/A♯7

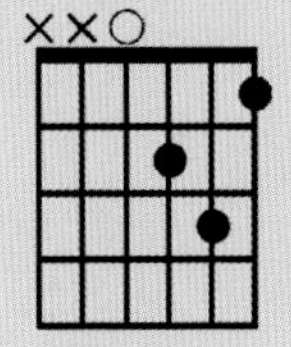

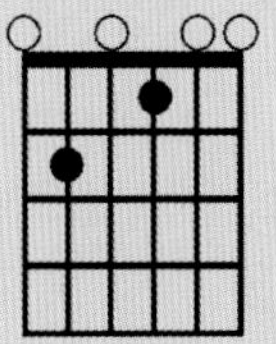

B♭/A♯ minor

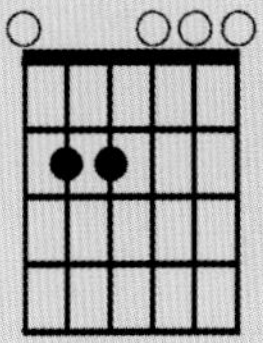

B♭/A♯m   E♭/D♯m   F7/E♯7

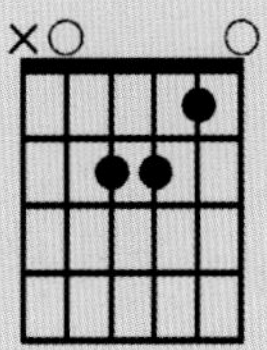

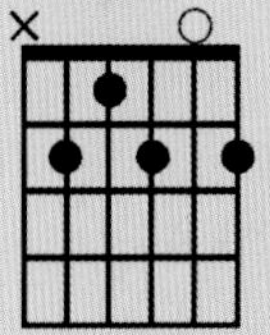

Capo keys:
seventh fret keys

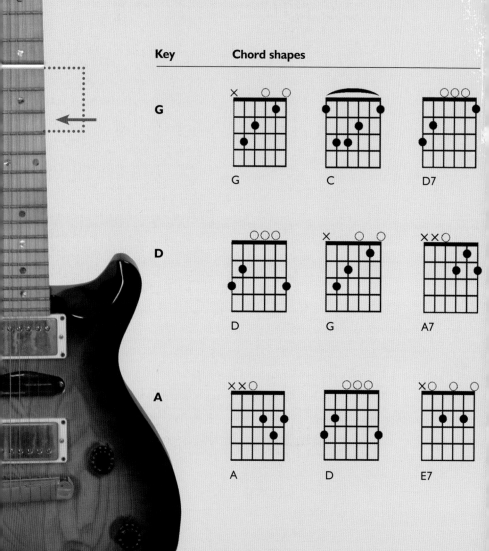

Key	Chord shapes

G

G C D7

D

D G A7

A

A D E7

Key	Chord shapes		

E

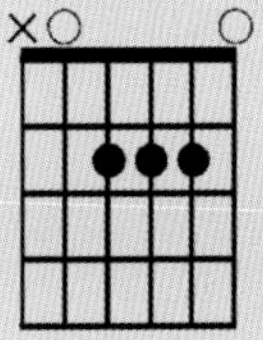

E   A   B7

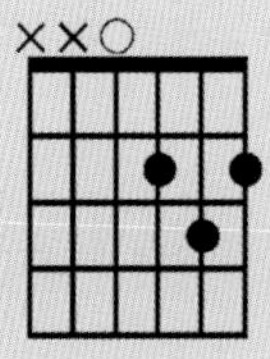

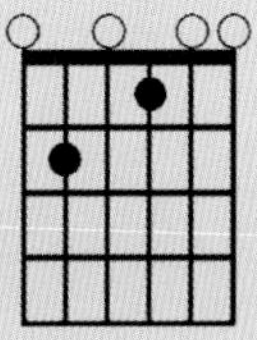

B

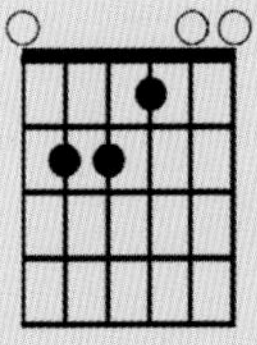

B   E   F#7

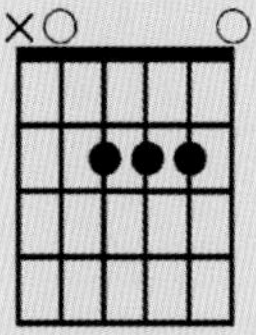

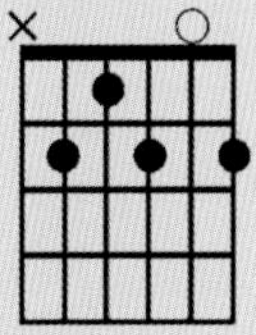

E minor

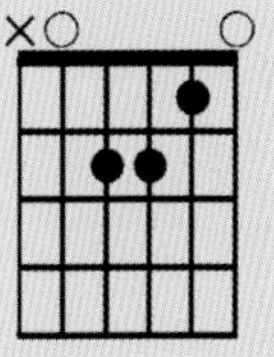

Em   Am   B7

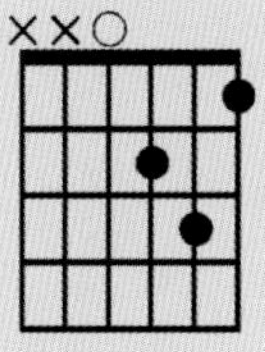

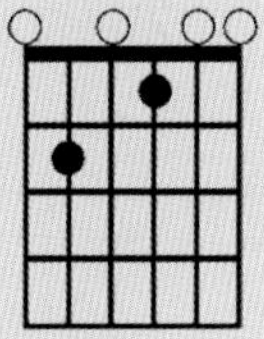

B minor

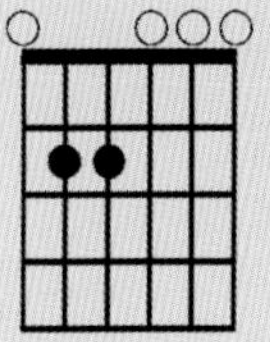

Bm   Em   F#7

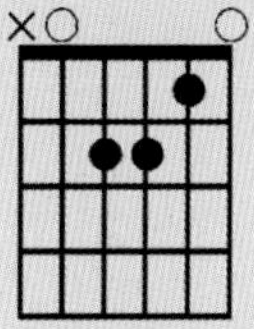

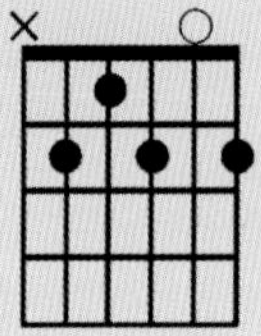

Capo keys:
eighth fret keys

Key	Chord shapes

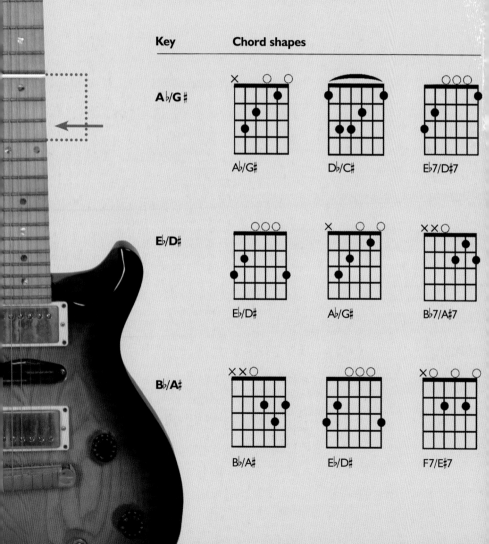

A♭/G♯

A♭/G♯　　Db/C♯　　E♭7/D♯7

E♭/D♯

E♭/D♯　　A♭/G♯　　B♭7/A♯7

B♭/A♯

B♭/A♯　　E♭/D♯　　F7/E♯7

Key	Chord shapes

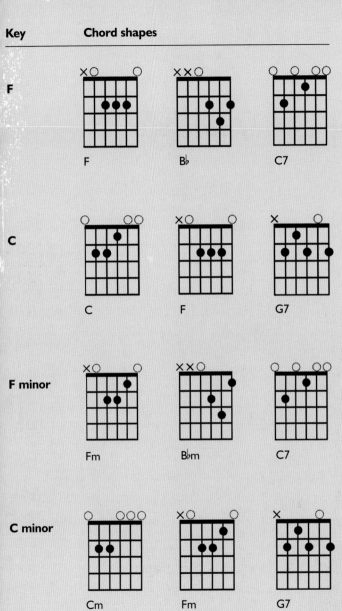

F

F   Bb   C7

C

C   F   G7

F minor

Fm   Bbm   C7

C minor

Cm   Fm   G7

Capo keys:
ninth fret keys

Key	Chord shapes		

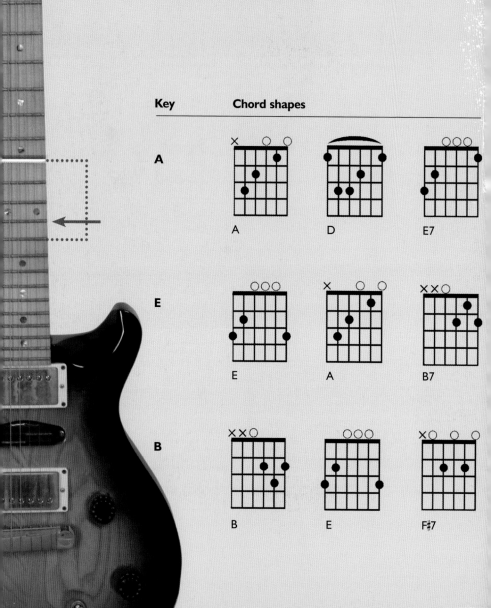

A

A   D   E7

E

E   A   B7

B

B   E   F#7

Key	Chord shapes

F#/G♭

F#/G♭   B/C♭   C#7/D♭7

C#/D♭

C#/D♭   F#/G♭   G#7/A♭7

F#/G♭ minor

F#/G♭m   B/C♭m   C#7/D♭7

C#/D♭ minor

C#/C♭m   G#/G♭m   G#7/A♭7

Glossary

Words shown in *italic* type have their own entry in the glossary.

arpeggiated Where the individual notes of a chord are picked out as opposed to being sounded simultaneously. The full chord shape should be held down throughout to allow the notes to ring into each other.

arpeggios Where the notes of a chord are played individually (but not allowed to ring into each other) as opposed to being sounded simultaneously. They are an invaluable tool for creating melodies and improvisations.

augmented chord A chord constructed by stacking two major third intervals on top of each other. This creates a major third and perfect fifth above the root note. Augmented chords are quite dissonant and usually occur as a V chord (i.e., in a perfect major or minor *cadence*).

backbeat A term used to describe the emphasis of the weak beats two and four (in 4/4 time) in popular music. This is usually emphasized by the drummer (and played on the snare drum), but is also reinforced by the rhythm guitarist.

barre chords By fretting across the strings with the first finger, and re-fingering an open chord shape in front of it, a *moveable chord shape*

is then created. The most common barre chords are type one (based on an open E chord) and type two (based on an open A chord).

cadence A term used to describe a concluding harmonic sequence. There are four basic types of cadence: Perfect (V–I), Plagal (IV–I), Imperfect (where the cadence ends on the V chord), and Interrupted (where the V chord resolves to a chord other than I).

comping A term used by musicians to describe an accompaniment or rhythm part, i.e., a blues-style "comp" would be a riff or chord-based accompaniment played by a guitarist over a 12-bar blues.

consonance An interval or chord is described as being "stable" when consonant. This is created by the series of harmonic overtones that are made when the notes are sounded simultaneously. A consonant chord or interval is used to release the tension created by dissonant chords and intervals.

contrary motion A musical term used to describe two melodic lines that move in opposite directions. The first three chords of the fingerpicked intro to "Stairway To Heaven" (Led Zeppelin) are a perfect example of contrary motion

(the lowest note of each chord moves down while the top note moves up).

damping When a string(s) is muted by quickly releasing the pressure of the fretting hand, or by touching the strings with the picking hand immediately after picking them.

diatonic This term is applied to any note, interval or chord that occurs naturally in a major or minor key (i.e., without requiring any scale note to be changed with a sharp, flat or natural).

diminished chord A chord constructed by stacking two minor third intervals on top of each other. This creates a minor third and diminished fifth above the *root note*. Diminished chords are quite dissonant and are frequently used as passing chords or to create tension.

dissonance The opposite of consonance, a dissonant chord or interval is said to be unstable. Dissonance is used to create motion in harmony by creating a need for resolution. This is described as "tension and release"; the dissonance provides tension, which is released when consonance occurs.

dominant seventh chord
A major *triad* with a fourth note added to a minor third above the fifth. This creates a minor seventh interval above the *root note*. The chord occurs diatonically on the fifth (V) degree of the major scale and resolves naturally to the scale's tonic (I) chord. It is a dissonant chord because of the diminished fifth interval between the major third and minor seventh.

fingerpicking The technique used to pluck the strings with the thumb and fingers, as opposed to using a pick or plectrum. It is a popular technique with solo guitarists because melody and accompaniment parts can be played simultaneously.

grace note Distinguishable from a regular note by a smaller print size (and usually with a line through the stem) in conventional notation, or by a smaller print size number in *TAB*. It is used to indicate the starting note of a non-rhythmical *hammer-on*, *pull-off* or *slide* and is played quickly just before the main note.

hammer-on When only the first of two notes on the same string is picked – the second is created solely by fretting the note sharply ("hammering" the finger onto the fretboard).

inversion A chord that has a note other than its *root note* as the lowest note. This is frequently the third or fifth, but can also be the seventh of a seventh chord.

legato A term that literally means to play smoothly or "tied together." In fingerstyle guitar this is achieved by picking only the first note (with the thumb or finger), the second pitch is generated with a *hammer-on* or *pull-off*.

let ring An instruction usually found at the beginning of a piece of music (in brackets) or under a specific section of music (indicated by a dashed line) to indicate that chords should be *arpeggiated*.

machine heads/tuning pegs
These are the adjustable knobs located on the guitar's headstock and are used to tension the strings. There is one tuning peg per string, enabling each string to be individually tuned.

major chord The major chord is the most consonant (i.e., stable) chord in music. It is a *triad* constructed from the first, third and fifth degrees of the major scale. Often described as a "happy-sounding" chord.

minor chord The minor chord is slightly less consonant (i.e., stable) than a *major chord* due to the relationship between the *root note* of the chord and the minor third. It is constructed from the first, third and fifth degrees of the harmonic minor scale. Often described as a "sad-sounding" chord.

moveable chord shape A non-open chord that does not incorporate open strings and so can be played anywhere on the neck. Moveable chords are extremely useful since they allow the guitarist to play in any key.

offbeat When counting in common time (4/4), the offbeats occur naturally between each beat. Counting "and" between the main beats will make it easier to locate the offbeats more accurately. A single bar of 4/4 would be counted as " 1 and 2 and 3 and 4 and."

open chord shape A chord played in first position (or with a capo higher up the neck) and using open strings. The five principal open chord shapes are C, A, G, E and D. Generally speaking, open chords are non-moveable.

ostinato A short melody or pattern that is constantly repeated, usually in the same part at the same pitch.

palm muting Where the heel of the picking hand palm is gently rested on the bass strings just in front of the guitar bridge. This creates semimuted bass notes. Used by many fingerstyle players to prevent the bass notes from overpowering the melody notes.

pickup measure/bar Used when the tune starts before the first bar (i.e., during the count in). A short (usually incomplete) bar precedes the first measure of the tune. A double barline will always follow a pickup measure (unless a repeat bar is used) to indicate the start of the first full measure.

pinch The process of playing two notes at the same time, achieved by picking with the thumb and a finger simultaneously.

power chord A guitar-specific, two-note chord that consists of a *root note* and a fifth. Sometimes the root note is doubled an octave higher to create a bigger sound. Since a power chord contains no third, it is neither major nor minor. "5" is used to denote a power chord (e.g. C5 = C power chord).

position This describes the position of the left hand on the fretboard. When playing in "first position," the first finger plays all notes on the first fret, the second finger all notes on the second fret, etc. So for "third position" the hand moves up the neck and the first finger now plays all notes on the third fret, the second finger plays notes on the fourth fret, etc.

pull-off A pull-off is created when only the first of two notes on the same string is picked – the second note is created by "flicking" the fretting finger slightly sideways as it is lifted off the string.

riff An *ostinato* (repeated) pattern, usually one or two bars in length and often played on the lower strings of the guitar. The introduction to "Smoke On The Water" is probably the most famous example of a guitar riff.

root note The note that a chord takes its name from (i.e., the note

A in an A major chord). This is usually, but not always, the lowest note of the chord.

scale A series of stepwise ascending (or descending) notes that follow a specific intervallic template of whole (*tone*) and half steps (*semitones*). These are generally seven notes long (i.e., the major scale), but can be shorter (i.e., the five note pentatonic), or longer (i.e., the eight note diminished scale).

seventh chord A major, minor, diminished or augmented *triad* with a fourth note added a third above the fifth interval (this can be either a major or minor third depending on the type of seventh desired). There are six basic seventh chord types: major seventh, dominant seventh, minor seventh, minor/major seventh, diminished seventh, and augmented seventh.

slide This is achieved by picking only the first note and then sliding the fretting finger up or down the neck to a new location. The fretting finger must maintain pressure on the fingerboard when sliding or the second note will not sound.

slur A slur is written above or below notes on the stave (as a curved line) to indicate *legato* phrasing. Guitar players achieve legato phrasing with the use of hammer-ons and pull-offs.

staccato A term used to describe notes that are played shorter than their written value. In fingerstyle

guitar this is achieved by releasing the pressure of your fretting hand to cut the note(s) short.

stave The stave or staff is a system of five lines used to denote pitch in conventional music notation. Specific symbols denote the length of each note or rest (silence).

syncopation The emphasis of "weak" beats to create an interesting rhythm. Weak beats occur on the second and fourth beat (in 4/4 time), or on an offbeat (i.e., occurring on the "and" between the main beats).

TAB Originally used to notate lute music during the Renaissance, this simplified form of notation indicates where a note should be played on the fretboard. It does not indicate note duration or rests (silence).

three-chord trick The process of creating an entire accompaniment for a song using the three primary chords I (tonic), IV (subdominant) and V (dominant). Many songs are based on these chords since they represent the principal harmonic movement in Western harmony.

tone/semitone The units used to measure the distance between two notes. A tone is equivalent to a whole step (two frets) and a semitone a half step (one fret).

triad The three notes that make up a major, minor, diminished or augmented chord. A triad is the result of two thirds stacked on top of each other.

Index

Page numbers in *italic* refer to illustrations of people.

A

accompaniments: easy 38–43
Aeolian mode 116
American folk style:
   picking pattern 184–5
"Andante in C" 168
arpeggiated chords 38, 250
arpeggios 250
augmented chords 250

B

"Babe I'm Gonna Leave You" 42
Bacharach, Burt 158
backbeat 250
Baez, Joan *19*, 38
Baldry, Long John 141
ballads: picking patterns 186–7,
   206–7, 219–22, 225, 229
barre chords 50–3, 250
   five-string 52
   four-string 53
   patterns 66–71
   six-string 51
basslines:
   alternating thumb 88–93
   damping 81, 90
   playing 26–9
   root and fifth 72–7
      country tune 78–87
   root/minor seventh 88–93
   walking 176–81
Beatles 42, 158, 168, *173*
beats: counting 30
Bibb, Eric 98
Bilk, Acker 109
"Blackbird" 168, *173*
bluegrass mountain music: picking
   pattern 202–3

blues 88
   classic albums 96–9
   minor scale 134
   picking patterns 186–7, 192–3,
      194–5, 212–13, 218–19, 223
   tune 94–101
bossa nova:
   accompaniments 152–7
   arrangement 158–67
   classic recordings 153
"The Boxer" 60
Brown, Joe 141
"The Bucket" 48
Byrd, Charlie *152*, 153

C

C major: harmonizing melody
   in 104–7
capo:
   keys available 231–49
Carthy, Martin 127
Cassidy, Eva 38
Charles, Ray 177
chord shapes:
   moveable 50–3, 251
      major seventh 150
   open 34–7, 251
chords:
   arpeggiated 38, 250
   augmented 250
   barre 50–3, 250
      patterns 66–71
   basic 34–7
   changing 41, 66
   diminished 250
   dominant: exotic 148, 151
   dominant seventh 34, 37,
      148, 251

inversions 34, 35, 36, 37
   learning 71
   major 34, 35, 251
      diatonic 102
      sevenths 150
   minor 34, 36, 148, 251
      adding to major harmony 107
      sevenths: finding 88
   Phrygian 50
   power 63, 252
   seventh 252
   tenths 168–75
Clapton, Eric 158
Collins, Judy 109
common time 43
   cut common 77
comping 250
compound time 43
concert pitch 20
consonance 250
contrary motion 54, 250
country music:
   picking patterns 186–7, 200–1,
      202–3, 208–9, 216, 219, 229
         Southern swing style 214–15
   tune 78–87
Cream 134
cut time (cut common) 77

D

damping 250
Davis, Miles 177
"Dear Prudence" 42
Deep Purple 134
Diamond, Neil 109
diatonic 250
   major chords 102
   minor chords 116

diminished chord 250
directory of picking patterns
    183–229
dissonance 250
dominant chords: exotic 148, 151
dominant seventh chords 34, 37,
    148, 251
        inversions 37
dots: reading 16–17
Dylan, Bob 38, 158

E
Eagles 60
eighth fret: capo keys 246–7
electronic tuner 20
Emmanuel, Tommy *135*
endings: first and second time 94

F
Faithfull, Marianne 127
Farjeon, Eleanor 109
fifth fret: capo keys 240–1
fifths 72–7
    finding 72
fingerboard:
    notes on 10–11
    repetition 10
fingering 162
fingerpicks: using 22
first fret: capo keys 232–3
folk music:
    American: picking pattern 184–5
    picking patterns 208–9, 229
fourth fret: capo keys 238–9
frets:
    capo keys 231–49
    notes on 10–11
Frusciante, John 168, *171*

G
"The Gallows Pole":
    arrangement 140–7
Garfunkel, Art 109
    see also Simon and Garfunkel

Getz, Stan 153
Gilberto, Joao 152, 153
"The Girl from Ipanema" 158
Giuliani, Mauro 168
grace notes 44, 251
guitar:
    holding 18–19
    left-handed 12
    right-handed: use by
        left-handed 12
Guthrie, Arlo 38

H
hammer-on 251
Hancock, Herbie 127
harmonizing:
    major melodies 102–7
        adding minor chords 107
    minor melodies 116–25
Hayward, Justin 127
Hendrix, Jimi 134, 158, 177
Hooker, John Lee 97
"Hotel California" 60
Howlin' Wolf 97
Hurt, Mississippi John *149*

I
interlude sections: picking patterns
    210–11, 228
intros: picking patterns 188–9,
    210–11, 222, 228
inversion 34, 35, 36, 37, 251

J
James, Eddie (Son House) *93*
jazz styles: picking pattern 224
Jobim, Antônio Carlos 152, 153,
    155, 158
Johnson, Robert 96, 134

K
King, BB 99
Kings of Leon 48

L
Latin American rhythms 152–7
Leadbelly 141
Led Zeppelin 42, 134, *140*,
    140, 141
Lee, Peggy 177, *177*
left hand: position 24–5
left-handed players 12
legato 101, 251
let ring 32, 38, 251

M
McCartney, Paul 12, *13*
machine heads 251
major chords 34, 35, 251
    diatonic 102
    inversions 35
    sevenths 148-50
        moveable shapes 150
    tenths 168
major melodies: harmonizing 102–7
melodies:
    major: harmonizing 102–7
    minor: harmonizing 116–25
melody notes: adding 30–3
Mendes, Sergio, & Brasil '66
    127, 127
metronome 28
Metté, Roy 141
minor blues scale 134
minor chords 34, 36, 251
    adding to major harmony 107
    commonly used 116
    diatonic 116
    inversions 36
    sevenths: finding 88
    tenths 168
minor melodies: harmonizing
    116–25
Mitchell, Joni 38, *103*
Mokhtar, Julian 141
Montgomery, Wes 127
"Morning Has Broken" 108–15
Morrison, Van 177

Mouskouri, Nana 109
moveable chord shapes 50–3, 251
  major seventh 150
Muddy Waters 96–7
muting: with palm 81, 90, 251

N
Neville, Aaron 109
ninth fret: capo keys 248–9
notation, conventional 16–17
  indicating fingering on 22
notes: length of 17

O
octaves 10
Odetta 141
offbeat 251
one-chord vamp: adding walking
  bassline 180
open chord shapes 34–7, 251
open strings 11
ornamentation 44
ostinato 251
outros: picking patterns 188–9, 228

P
Paisley, Brad 79
palm muting 81, 90, 251
pedal note 68
Phrygian chord 50
picking pattern directory 183–229
pickup bar 78, 251–2
"Pinball Wizard" 48
pinching 30, 31, 252
pop music: picking patterns 196–7,
  198–9, 219–22
posture 18–19
power chords 63, 252
"Purple Haze" 134

R
Radiohead 68
rallentando 65
Red Hot Chili Peppers 168

riffs 134–9, 252
right hand: position of 22–3
right-handed guitars: use by
  left-handers 12
ringing 32, 38, 57
Ritter, Tex 141
rock music:
  picking patterns 196–7,
    204–5, 226
    classic 188–9
    pop/rock 198–9, 220–1
    rock 'n' roll 214–15
Rogers, Kenny 109
Rolling Stones 134
root note 252
root/fifths bassline 72–7
root/minor seventh bassline 88–93

S
scales 252
  minor blues 134
"Scarborough Fair":
  accompaniment 126–33
second fret: capo keys 234–5
Seeger, Pete 38
semiquaver:
  patterns 60–5
  picking pattern 67
semitone 252
seventh chords 252
  dominant 34, 37, 148, 251
  major 148–50
  minor 88, 148
seventh fret: capo keys 244–5
Shaw, Martin 109
shuffle 93
Simon, Paul 38
Simon and Garfunkel 60, 126,127
Sinatra, Frank 153
singer-songwriter music: picking
  patterns 190–1, 206–7, 217, 227
sixth fret: capo keys 242–3
slurs 44, 252
"Smoke on the Water" 134

staccato 101, 252
stave 252
  five-line 16–17
Stevens, Cat 109
strings: open 11
"Sunshine of Your Love" 134
swamp rock: picking pattern 186–7
syncopation 30, 32, 252
  combined with pinching 30, 33
    patterns 44–9

T
TAB 252
  reading 16-17
Tales of the Riverbank theme 168
Taylor, James 38, 121
tenths: playing 168–75
third fret: capo keys 236–7
three-chord trick 252
thumbpicks: using 22, 23
time signatures:
  2/2 77, 144
  4/4 77
  6/8 43
  12/8 93, 137
tone 252
transposing patterns 54–9
triads 34, 252
tritone 34
tuning 20–1
tuning pegs (machine heads) 251
turnaround 40

V
vamping: one-chord: adding walking
  bassline 180

W
Walker, T-Bone 98
walking basslines 176–81
Waters, Muddy 96–7
The Who 48

Credits

Quarto would like to thank the following agencies for kindly supplying images for inclusion in this book:

pp. 13, 19, 93, 135, 140, 149, 152, 155, 171, 173 Getty Images
pp. 79, 103, 121 Rex Features
p. 126 Corbis

We would also like to thank:

p. 97 copyright © 2010 SONY MUSIC ENTERTAINMENT
p. 98 Geffen Records
p. 109bl Laserlight
pp. 109, 127, 153 A&M Records
p. 141 Country Stars; Polygram Int'l